Your Older Dog

Your Older Dog

*A Complete Guide to Helping Your
Dog Live a Longer and Healthier Life*

Jean Callahan

**A Fireside Book
Published by Simon & Schuster**

NEW YORK   LONDON   TORONTO   SYDNEY   SINGAPORE

FIRESIDE
Rockefeller Center
1230 Avenue of the Americas
New York, NY 10020

FIRESIDE and colophon are registered
trademarks of Simon & Schuster, Inc.

Printed in China

10 9 8 7 6 5 4 3 2 1

Library of Congress Cataloging-in-
Publication Data is available.

ISBN 0-7432-0309-7

Photography:

Cover Image: Ted Schiffman
Regina Grenier: 24, 33, 51, 54, 105, 127
Patricia Hanifey: 47
Devon Hildreth: 12, 69, 131
Gail Smith: 22, 87, 108, 125
Photodisc: 1, 3, 6, 7, 8, 10, 14, 16, 19, 20,
            25, 26, 31, 34, 36, 37,
            41, 49, 53, 66, 75, 79,
            81, 88, 91, 92, 93, 97,
            102, 107, 110, 112,
            113, 115, 119, 121,
            123, 133

Illustration: Todd Bonita
            tmbonita@aol.com

Layout by SYP Design & Production
            www.sypdesign.com

To Hobo, Amigo,
Rico, Pumpkin, and Southie

CONTENTS

BY

ANNE MARIE MANNING, D.V.M.

From the time we choose our dogs until the inevitable moment they depart our company, we are rewarded with a relationship unlike any other. Regardless of why we choose to bring a dog into our lives, we are graced with a constant friend, companion, playmate, confidant, and family member. Dogs are one of life's gifts and lessons together in one fur-covered package. Our bond with our pets is a gift, and the responsibility of loving, caring, and providing for them can apply to all of our human relationships.

From the day we bring a dog into our home, whether it is weeks old or years old, we are responsible for providing food, shelter, medical care and, most importantly, love. Not only do we need to attend to their basic needs, we have to train and socialize them properly so that their relationships with us and other animals are successful. They, in turn, teach us patience and understanding as is required when they chew our shoes, soil the new carpet, dig holes in the yard, or pretend they don't hear us call. They also reward us with their never-ending happiness, eagerness, curiosity, and joy as we watch them learn and grow.

Throughout their time with us, our dogs provide us with endless companionship.

They are so in tune with our feelings that when we are happy, they celebrate with us by bounding at our feet, barking, or waiting with expectation for our next move. And when we are anxious or sad, they are ready to offer their head to be petted or to leap into our laps to provide comfort and warmth. It is our dogs' straightforward approach to life that teaches us that the most important things in our own lives may very well be a good meal, someone to love, and time to play and relax.

As our dogs grow old, they may develop age-related medical problems or experience behavioral changes, and when this happens, we'll change our pace to accommodate their needs: slower leash walks, administering medications with meals, lifting them in and out of the car or off the couch to lessen the impact on arthritic joints. Watching a pet age is perhaps the most difficult experience in our relationship with them. As long as their life span is shorter than ours, it will always seem that we have never had enough time with them. Even in death our pets teach us life's lessons. It is possible to die with grace and dignity, it is normal and okay to grieve the passing of a loved one, and eventually grief will lessen and we will be left with the knowledge that our memories of years spent with loved ones never fade.

LIVING LONGER AND
LIVING BETTER

Dogs have been our faithful companions for more than 15,000 years. Archeologists have found the remains of domesticated wolves, our dogs' ancestors, in their explorations of prehistoric human settlements. Those ancient wolf-dogs worked hard as protectors and hunters. Of course, dogs' lives are quite different today. Valued for their loyalty, their devoted friendship, their big trusting eyes, and their unconditional love, dogs are beloved members of our families.

Because we dote on our dogs, they live longer. Better veterinary care and improved nutrition have increased the canine life span from an average of seven years in the 1930s to twelve years today. And with the right care, it's not at all uncommon for dogs to live to fourteen, fifteen, or even twenty years old these days. Sixty-one percent of American homes have pets, and 54 million of these pets are dogs. Our dogs live such good lives, in fact, that, like their owners, they are often challenged by unhealthy habits associated with affluence: rich diets, too many treats, and insufficient exercise. Also, the inevitable aches and pains that are a natural part of living to a ripe old age present challenges for dogs as well as their owners.

We develop strong attachments to dogs who share our homes for so many years. In a recent survey, 57 percent of dog owners polled said that if they were stranded on a desert island, they would choose pets over spouses or other humans for companionship. Almost 80 percent said that they give their pets holiday or birthday presents, while 62 percent sign letters or cards from themselves and their pets. And 55 percent think of themselves as parents to their puppies.

Devoted is an adjective that describes dog owners as well as the dogs themselves. The more chronological and emotional history we share, the stronger the bond between human and animal becomes. You are devoted to your dog and want to do everything you can to maximize the best years of your dog's life. That's why you're reading this book. By learning about preventive health care and treatment of common ailments, you can help your dog live longer and feel better.

Aging is not the inevitable beginning of sickness and suffering. Older dogs can enjoy many years of active life when owners pay attention to their changing health needs. This book will focus on the changing needs of dogs beginning at age seven. Although dogs enter old age at different rates, most start to become vulnerable to the major and minor problems associated with aging at around seven years old. Like forty or fifty for humans, seven marks the onset of mid-life in the canine species.

HOW DOGS HELP US

Dogs don't care how old or handsome or pretty you are, or what kind of car you drive, or how much money you make. Canine companions are nonjudgmental, loyal, and devoted. The bond between pets and their people is so powerful that it contributes to our mental, emotional, and physical well-being. In fact, a 1999 study showed that a pet's calming influence works better at controlling high blood pressure than the most frequently used prescription drugs. Another study, published in 1992, showed that pet owners are less likely than people who don't own pets to develop heart disease. A 1980 study found that pet owners who have heart attacks live longer than heart attack victims who don't have pets. Finally, researchers at the University of California at Davis and at UCLA have found that people of all ages who have pets visit their doctors less often, have more fun, and feel more secure than people who don't.

Dogs have always been hard workers. Guiding blind people through city streets, herding animals on farms, and guarding homes and property are some of the better known canine professions, but recently, dogs have been branching out into new fields. They're dropping in at nursing homes and hospitals, where, as studies have shown, their visits help patients heal faster with less need for pain-killing medicines. They're going to school with teachers who have found that a dog's presence in the classroom actually lowers truancy rates and improves test scores. Canine love and devotion can even help autistic children and children with attention deficit hyperactivity disorder tune in to the outside world with less anxiety.

Organizations like Pet Partners, a national group devoted to promoting the human-animal bond, arranges for volunteers to bring their pets into hospitals and schools. In Washington state, dogs are even going to prison! At a state prison for women felons, service dogs are raised and trained by inmates under the Prison Pet Partnership Program, an offshoot of Pet Partners. These dogs will eventually serve people who are blind, deaf, or wheel-chair- or homebound. During the six-to-eight-month training period, dogs live in the cells with their trainers, who groom them and train them using positive rein-forcement. When the inmates have served out their sen-tences, they not only leave prison with a new job skill, but they have learned a lot about themselves. Not one of the women who has participated in the Prison Pet Partnership Program since it started in 1988 has been a repeat offender.

THE DISCREET CHARMS OF THE OLDER DOG

While some dogs serve people by performing specific tasks, such as helping individuals with special needs, others simply curl up by the fire or on the sofa and make everybody in the house feel comforted by their presence. Since older dogs are calmer and wiser than young pups, their gifts for soothing spirits are unique. Older dogs can make sweet companions for older people. Their visits to nursing homes and assisted living facili-ties are particularly well-received because older dogs enjoy sitting still for good, long petting sessions. Older dogs can also be ideal playmates for young children. Because they are already house-trained and need less exercise, they make wonderful pets for busy people who don't have the time or energy for a younger animal. Whether you have recently adopted your older dog or whether he or she has been part of your family for years, you know how lucky you are to be the human companion of an older dog.

Top Ten Reasons to Love Older Dogs

1. They let you get a good night's sleep: they don't need midnight snacks or bathroom runs.

2. Older dogs are less demanding than younger dogs: they leave you time for yourself.

3. Older dogs know who they are: they're grown-ups with real personalities.

4. They're constant companions: they stay by your side on walks in the park.

5. Older dogs love to sit and be petted for as long as you want to pet them.

6. They've learned what it takes to get along and they know how to be part of a pack.

7. Older dogs know what "no" means.

8. They can learn new tricks: older dogs focus better because they're more relaxed.

9. Because they're not teething, older dogs won't chew your favorite slip-pers to bits.

10. They're housebroken.

HOW YOUR DOG AGES

Older dogs can enjoy many years of active life when owners pay attention to their changing health needs.

CHAPTER ONE

the aging process

Most of us are only too aware of our own aging process. Almost as soon as we're past adolescence, we note tiny laugh lines around our eyes and other subtle hints that our beautiful bodies really are subject to the laws of gravity. Midlife brings significant changes. Our bodies thicken here, soften there, and don't respond quite as reliably as they once did. Eyesight and hearing start to fail. Our hair grays, and in some cases, falls out. We gain weight when we even look at food. And that cheerful, ready-for-anything attitude of youth tends to fade. We become more cautious about taking risks, maybe even a little crotchety and set in our ways. Although these changes can be difficult to detect in the early stages, they are all occurring in our faithful canine companions, too.

The older dog's coat becomes thinner and dryer. Hair on the muzzle and around the ears turns gray. Muscles shrink and the body gradually becomes weaker. Hearing deteriorates, resulting in deafness in some dogs. Eyesight weakens. Many middle-aged dogs develop cloudy lenses in the eyes that could be the beginnings of cataracts. Dogs put on weight eating the same diet that kept them trim as pups, or they lose interest in regular meals and are constantly begging for treats. The dog that couldn't wait to go out and run last year is slowing down, perhaps even whining in protest of a morning walk on cold days. He's taking the stairs one at a time instead of in leaps and bounds. And, he can be cranky, too, intolerant of toddlers who want to play with him and less responsive to your commands and your affection.

HOW AND WHY DOGS AGE

Scientists have developed many theories to explain aging in humans and other mammals, but no one really knows how and why it happens. According to one theory, the cells of all living beings contain a built-in genetic program, a DNA clock that sets the pace of aging and determines the outer limits of each being's life span from birth. It's as if each body contains a fixed amount of energy that slowly dissipates over time and is finally used up. Other scientists blame the aging process on the hardships of daily life — cells are damaged by toxins in the foods we eat and the air we breathe, and by the gradual, inevitable wear and tear on our bodies that is just a part of living. These scientists compare this wear and tear to the rusting out that happens to the bodies of old cars. Still other biologists believe that the fault lies with our immune systems. They contend that as time takes its toll, our immune systems gradually wear out, and our bodies become more susceptible to infection and disease.

Like people, dogs are individual in the way they age. Certain breeds, mixed breeds, and, in general, smaller dogs tend to live longer. According to Tufts University School of Veterinary Medicine, one of the most respected veterinary colleges in the United States, the point at which a dog enters the golden years varies, although age seven is about average. (This roughly corresponds to the 55-plus category in people.) Tufts University veterinarians generally consider small dogs to be senior citizens at about twelve years of age, while large dogs reach the senior stage at six to eight years of age. Therefore, a Chihuahua or a dachshund might not show serious signs of age until she is twelve or so, while a cocker spaniel or a fox terrier may not start to seem old until about age ten. But larger dogs, such as Great Danes or golden retrievers, usually begin to show their age sooner — by age eight or nine.

How Size Affects the Aging Process

Giant breeds (such as a St. Bernard)	Average life span: 7 to 10 years Enters senior stage: 5 to 7 years	
Large breeds (such as a Samoyed)	Average life span: 8 to 12 years Enters senior stage: 6 to 8 years	
Medium breeds (such as a terrier)	Average life span: 12 to 15 years Enters senior stage: 7 to 9 years	
Small breeds (such as a Bichon Frise)	Average life span: up to 15 years Enters senior stage: 9 to 11 years	

The Aging Process: Human Years and Dog Years

Although life expectancy varies considerably among breeds, and smaller dogs tend to age more slowly than big dogs, you can generally measure your dog's age equivalent in human years using the chart below. After two years of age, one year equals four human years.

COMPARATIVE AGES OF DOGS AND HUMANS

Dogs	Humans
3 months	5 years
6 months	10 years
1 year	15 years
4 years	32 years
8 years	48 years
15 years	76 years

WHAT CAN YOU DO TO HELP?

Start paying close attention to your dog's aging process as he reaches middle age. Some changes are preventable; others are not. As your dog gets older, two types of changes will occur: age-related changes and true illnesses. Age-related changes are more diffi- cult to prevent. These changes, such as hearing and visual impairment, are normal and will eventually develop in most animals. But, with optimum care, they can be postponed for years and their effects can be minimized.

Life Expectancy

What's the average life expectancy of your dog?

BREED	LIFE EXPECTANCY	BREED	LIFE EXPECTANCY
Afghan Hound	12 – 14 years	Irish Terrier	13 years
Airedale	13 years	Irish Wolfhound	11 years
Akita	10 – 12 years	Jack Russell Terrier	13 – 14 years
Alaskan Malamute	12 years	Labrador Retriever	12 – 14 years
American Foxhound	11 – 13 years	Lhasa Apso	13 – 14 years
American Water Spaniel	12 years	Maltese	14 – 15 years
Basset Hound	12 years	Mastiff	10 – 12 years
Beagle	13 years	Norwegian Elkhound	12 – 13 years
Bernese Mountain Dog	10 – 12 years	Papillon	13 – 15 years
Bichon Frise	14 years	Pekingese	12 – 13 years
Bloodhound	10 – 12 years	Pembroke Welsh Corgi	12 – 14 years
Border Collie	12 – 14 years	Pit Bull Terrier	12 years
Borzoi (Russian Wolfhound)	11 – 13 years	Pomeranian	15 years
Boston Terrier	13 years	Portuguese Water Dog	12 – 14 years
Boxer	12 years	Rhodesian Ridgeback	12 years
Bull Terrier	11 – 13 years	Rottweiller	11 – 12 years
Cairn Terrier	14 years	Saluki	12 years
Cardigan Welsh Corgi	12 – 14 years	Samoyed	12 years
Chesapeake Bay Retriever	12 – 13 years	Scottish Terrier	13 – 14 years
Chihhuaha	12 – 14 years	Shar Pei	11 – 12 years
Chow Chow	11 – 12 years	Shih Tzu	13 – 14 years
Cocker Spaniel	13 – 14 years	Siberian Husky	11 – 13 years
Collie	12 – 14 years	St. Bernard	11 years
Dachshund	14 – 17 years	Standard Poodle	11 – 15 years
Dalmation	12 – 14 years	Weimaraner	12 – 13 years
Doberman	12 years	Welsh Terrier	14 years
German Shepherd	12 – 13 years	West Highland White Terrier	14 years
Golden Retriever	13 – 15 years	Wheaten Terrier	13 – 14 years
Great Dane	10 years	Whippet	13 – 14 years
Grey Hound	10 – 12 years	Wire Fox Terrier	13 – 14 years
Irish Setter	13 years	Yorkshire Terrier	14 years

Illness is another story. Don't ignore the subtle signs of illness or dismiss them as normal aging. While there are many things you can do at home to help diagnose and treat the minor health problems of your older dog with preventive care, natural remedies, and first aid techniques—which you will read about in later chapters—there are times when only a professional veterinarian can diagnose and treat a disease. Never hesitate to take your older dog to the vet whenever he's not looking or feeling well for more than a day or two. With recent advances in veterinary medicine, many of the diseases your aging dog faces can be prevented or successfully treated.

Keep a close eye on your older pet. Picking up on the subtle changes that take place in the earliest stages of a disease can help prevent serious problems from developing. Even if a problem can't be cured, it can often be managed in such a way that your dog enjoys many more years of active, pain-free living and you enjoy many more years of companionship.

Healthy Dog Check List

Dogs, like people, sometimes need special care when they grow older. Mobility, eyesight, hearing, and other functions may be reduced to some degree or lost altogether. Regular veterinary checkups are an excellent way to keep tabs on your older dog's health. Good home care is also crucial. The following is a list of things you can check at home. Depending on your dog's age and health condition, you may want to run through this checklist once a week or a once a month. Make photocopies of this page to use for your frequent health checks. Date the health checks and keep them in a file or binder as a record to help you remember symptoms and dates when you visit the veterinarian.

- Appetite normal—no problems chewing or swallowing

- Drinks normal amounts of water

- Nose moist and free of discharge

- Teeth clean and free of tartar build-up—no bad breath

- Gums pink and moist with no redness or growths

- Eyes bright, clear, and free of matter

- Ears clean with no discharge, odor, or swelling

- Breathes without difficulty or excessive panting

- Coat shiny with no flaking or hair loss

- Skin free from itching or areas of irritation

- No lumps or bumps on the body

- No fleas, ticks, or mites

- Walks without stiffness, pain, or difficulty

- Urinates with usual frequency and has regular bowel movements which are normnal in size and consistency

- No slips in house training

CHAPTER TWO

age-related changes

As your dog gets older, you can expect visible changes. That distinguished bit of white around the muzzle, dryer skin, and a less lustrous coat are sure signs of aging. You will probably see shifts in appetite and changes in the senses of sight, smell, and taste, too. Your dog may sleep for more hours at night and take longer, more frequent naps during the day. Bit by bit, you will notice changes in his energy level. He'll be strolling, instead of bounding, on your daily walks. His gait may change, too. The dog who once thrilled at every butterfly that passed and jumped to attention the moment you called his name will gradually become less attentive and slower to respond. At the same time, he may develop greater sensitivity to stress.

FROM HEAD TO TAIL: AN OVERVIEW OF HOW YOUR OLDER DOG AGES

The easiest way to understand the changes your dog goes through as she ages is to take a look at what actually happens in each of her body systems.

THE EYES

A gradual weakening of vision is not abnormal in older dogs. Some breeds even suffer from inherited disorders that interfere with vision. If your dog begins bumping into furniture or hesitates before moving around in an unfamiliar environment, impaired vision could be the problem.

Dogs share some eye diseases with humans. One of them, cataracts, is a potentially serious age-related eye problem. In both humans and dogs, cataracts can lead to reduced vision and even blindness. Cataracts can be treated surgically. Older dogs may also develop glaucoma, an increase in pressure within the eye. When the white part (sclera) of an older dog's eye becomes red-tinged, the problem could be glaucoma. Glaucoma and cataracts frequently develop at the same time. Don't delay treatment for glaucoma. See your veterinarian as soon as you notice symptoms. Medical or surgical treatments may be needed to reduce the pressure in the eye and to treat any other disease.

One specific age-related vision problem is nuclear sclerosis. In this disease, the lens of the dog's eye becomes whitish and cloudy. Owners often worry when they see a milky lens and believe that the dog is developing cataracts. But, more often, the problem is nuclear sclerosis, which does not create serious vision problems. Dogs with nuclear sclerosis do have difficulty seeing at night, however, and can also find it difficult to focus on nearby objects.

THE EARS

You call your dog and she doesn't answer. A dog that usually leaps into action at your every command suddenly seems to be ignoring you. Do you have a canine mutiny on your hands?

Perhaps, but it's much more likely that you are dealing with an age-related hearing loss. Most older dogs cope pretty well with minor hearing impairments, without any medical intervention. They're smart enough to adapt, responding to hand signals and body language. Although a minor hearing loss won't keep your older dog from having a full and happy life, it's still a good idea to pay special attention. If you don't already keep your dog on a leash when you go out for walks, start doing so now. She may need that extra precaution to protect her from automobiles and other dangers.

Sometimes older dogs develop other ear problems. Ear mites are one of the most common canine ear troubles and older dogs are particularly susceptible. If you suspect mites, lift up your dog's earflap and look inside. You won't see the microscopic mites themselves but you will see their brownish-black droppings caked in your dog's ear. Dogs can also get bacterial or yeast infections in the ear. A dog who keeps trying to scratch at an ear may have an irritation or inflammation within the ear or of the skin surrounding the area. Like humans, a dog's sense of balance is tied in with inner ear mechanisms. A dog who stumbles or seems shaky on his feet may be suffering from an ear infection or an inner ear problem.

NOSE AND THROAT

Older dogs who sneeze and cough may be contending with more than a cold. As dogs get older, their lungs and bronchial tubes can begin to produce too much mucus, causing them to sneeze and cough inordinately. Veterinarians note that this is a particular problem with smaller dogs.

A nagging cough can be the first sign of bronchitis, an inflammation of the bronchial airways, which can develop quickly and become a chronic problem for some older

dogs. Mild cases may clear up by themselves, but when a cough persists for more than two weeks, a trip to the vet is recommended. A cough that persists can be a sign of serious diseases, including heart disease, heartworm infection, and cancer. But in most cases the cause is more benign and the veterinarian can treat the problem with a prescription for antibiotics or other medications. In rare instances, emphysema can develop as the lung tissue loses its elasticity.

Kennel cough, or canine infectious tracheobronchitis, is a common problem for older dogs. A highly infectious condition, kennel cough gets its name because it spreads rapidly among dogs who are boarding in kennels. Characterized by a harsh, dry, unproductive cough, kennel cough is seldom a serious disease. Most dogs recover without treatment within seven to fourteen days.

Because of differences in their physiological makeup, dogs do not develop asthma, an allergic condition that plagues felines and causes serious health problems for many humans.

Pneumonia is most likely to occur in very young or very old dogs. It is an inflammation of the lungs, caused by viral or bacterial infections. Symptoms include rapid, shallow breathing, coughing, listlessness, poor appetite, and fever. A dog with signs of pneumonia should be taken to the veterinarian right away. The veterinarian will take x-rays and administer blood tests to diagnose this disease. Treatment with antibiotics, and sometimes oxygen and drugs to aid breathing, are essential.

MOUTH

Farmers judge the age of a horse by looking into her mouth. Well, the same test could be applied to dogs. The mouth—and especially the teeth—reveal early signs of aging.

Has your dog's sparkling smile lost pizzazz? Is his breath, never minty-fresh, turned downright awful? Deteriorating gums and teeth could be the root of the problem. Veterinarians recommend good home care (daily brushing) and semiannual dental cleanings for dogs today—the same regimen that dentists recommend for humans. When dog owners don't keep up with their dog's teeth, gradually those pearly whites turn yellow and even brown.

Many older dogs have accumulated many years' worth of brown tartar and scale on their teeth. At this stage, a renewed commitment to good dental hygiene will usually remedy the problem. But when reddish, swollen, bleeding gums appear, more serious disease may be involved. Periodontal (gum) disease is just as much a problem for dogs as it is for humans. Periodontal disease can lead to loss of appetite and weight loss as chewing becomes painful. Neglected for too long, periodontal infections can spread to other parts of the body and contribute to the development of heart disease and kidney problems.

HEART AND CIRCULATORY SYSTEM

Carnivorous creatures that they are, very few dogs express much interest in heart-healthy diets. But, unlike humans, our lucky dogs seldom develop hardening of the arteries and other cardiovascular problems related to a rich, fatty diet. Dogs rarely suffer strokes, but they are susceptible to heart attacks as they get older.

The most common age-related cardiac disease dogs develop is congestive heart failure, resulting from problems with heart valves or infections in the bloodstream. Heart valve problems can often be traced to injuries when dogs are wounded in fights, or to the long-term effects of periodontal disease. Bloodstream infections

can create scar tissue on the valves, altering their shape and interfering with their proper functioning. Generally, smaller breeds are more prone to heart disease than larger dogs.

Older dogs can also develop anemia, a disease in which a shortage of red blood cells restricts the flow of oxygen through the body. A dog who seems tired all the time and has pale gums may be suffering from anemia. A mild case of anemia can be treated at home with a diet rich in iron and B vitamins (your veterinarian can recommend good food choices). There are also prescription and over-the-counter medicines available for the treatment of this disease. Once your veterinarian has diagnosed anemia, he or she will prescribe the right medicine for your dog.

Dogs of any age are susceptible to heartworm, a parasitic infection spread by mosquitoes. Dogs who are outdoors most of the time are more apt to get heartworm than dogs who live inside. A mild case of heartworm may show no symptoms at all; as the disease progresses, signs such as fatigue, aversion to exercise, and a cough can develop. Left untreated, heartworm can develop complications including hypertension, heart failure, liver or kidney disease. Veterinarians can treat this disease with drugs, but the best treatment is prevention. Most veterinarians include preventive heartworm treatment—in season or year round—as part of a dog's regular care.

As dogs age, their hearts work less efficiently. Inefficient pumping of the heart leads to decreased cardiac output, which, in turn, can lead to congestive heart failure. The first sign of congestive heart failure may be something as simple as a mild cough, so, it's important to take all coughs seriously.

Changes That Warrant Immediate Action

Most of the changes an older dog goes through are absolutely normal, but some changes are less than benign. The following symptoms could be a sign of serious disease and should never be ignored. See your vet as soon as possible if your older dog is exhibiting these symptoms:

❧ Sudden loss of weight.

❧ Serious loss of appetite to the point that your dog is eating almost nothing for several days.

❧ Diarrhea or vomiting which lasts more than a day can be a sign of many problems. A brief bout is usually just a reaction to a bad meal, but diarrhea that persists could be a symptom of distemper, pancreatitis, or diabetes. Persistent vomiting could be a sign of kidney, liver, or brain disease. Call the veterinarian immediately if diarrhea or vomiting continues longer than twenty-four hours or seems unusual in any way. Vomiting accompanied by staggering, weakness, and disorientation could mean a dog has been poisoned. When you see symptoms like these, get the dog to the veterinarian right away.

❧ Increase in appetite without increase in weight may mean diabetes. Ask the vet to run a blood test.

❧ Increased thirst, without a change in activity level, and increased urination are also signs of diabetes. Get your dog tested as soon as possible.

❧ Tiredness and fatigue when exercising is natural as a dog ages. Continue an exercise program, but modify it so that you don't overtax your dog: expecting too much could lead to falls and broken bones. But when your dog is tired and fatigued without exercising, it's time to see the vet.

❧ Difficulty in getting up from a lying position or other problems with moving may indicate arthritis. Ask the vet for advice on treatments and on ways you can relieve your dog's discomfort and labored mobility.

❧ Coughing and excessive panting may indicate heart, lung, or respiratory disease. First modify your dog's exercise program. If these symptoms persist, consult your veterinarian.

❧ Problems with vision or hearing are to be expected as your dog enters the senior years. Accommodate these changes as best you can. Keep furniture where your dog expects it to be, for example, or clap instead of calling your dog's name when he no longer seems able to hear you.

❧ Abnormal behavior—for instance, roaming in circles, barking at nothing, being withdrawn, having "accidents" in the house—may be indicators of illness, disease, or cognitive dysfunction. See your vet right away.

LIVER, KIDNEYS, AND URINARY TRACT

Like aging humans, older dogs often feel the weight of the years as wear and tear on their organs and body systems. The liver, a vital organ that helps your dog metabolize the food she eats and detoxify her blood, may become less efficient in her later years. Early signs of liver disease include loss of appetite, weight loss, and frequent drinking and urination. Left untreated, an impaired liver can develop into serious medical problems, such as jaundice and spontaneous internal bleeding.

Kidney function also declines as dogs age. Your dog will probably need to urinate more frequently. Also, it's important to feed her nutritious food and provide plenty of fresh water to keep the kidneys working at an optimal level. In some cases, restricting salt intake and limiting protein to high quality sources may also be necessary. Your veterinarian will advise you on these issues.

The kidneys are part of the urinary tract along with the ureters, bladder, and, in male dogs, the prostrate and urethra. The main symptom of urinary tract problems, other than kidney disease, is trouble with voiding— painful urination, excessive urination, and urinary incontinence are the most common. Because symptoms overlap and more than one organ is involved, it is usually necessary for the veterinarian to run tests on urine specimens and blood samples to determine what's causing such problems.

NERVOUS SYSTEM

The brain, the spinal cord, and the nerves that run throughout the body comprise your dog's nervous system. In your dog's younger years, the greatest threat to his nervous system came from traumatic injury. That threat remains, but, as he ages, your dog may also become vulnerable to other problems. Fortunately, dogs seldom suffer from brain tumors or strokes, and hereditary nervous diseases are uncommon. When hereditary diseases do occur, they usually show up at birth or in the early years of a dog's life. Dogs can develop seizure disorders, such as epilepsy. Although these conditions are frightening when first diagnosed, veterinarians have an arsenal of powerful drugs available for the treatment of seizure disorders.

Some older dogs also develop a condition called cognitive dysfunction disorder (see behavioral problems on page 34). This disease causes changes in the brain that limit mental faculties such as thinking, recognition, memory, and learned behavior. Cognitive dysfunction is a progressive disease, much like Alzheimer's disease in humans. Also like Alzheimer's, there is currently no cure. However, veterinarians can prescribe medication that significantly improves symptoms and enhances quality of life.

DIGESTIVE SYSTEM

Expect appetite changes as your dog ages. Whether your older dog eats more or less, she may not be getting all the nutrition she needs from the food she's used to eating.

Older dogs' digestive systems gradually wear down. Their ability to absorb the nutrients in the food they eat isn't as top-notch as it was when they were pups. As dogs' senses of taste, hearing, smell, and sight are all decreased, food seems less appealing. Some dogs eat less and lose weight. Otheres, slowed down by age, are bored so they eat more, exercise less, and gain weight.

Combine digestive problems with the decreased liver function that sometimes accompanies old age and what you get could be malnutrition. It's important to feed your dog high-quality food as he gets older. You may even want to supplement his diet with vitamins and minerals. There are many senior dog food choices today. You

can also prepare wholesome, homemade food without too much difficulty. We will explore all these options in the nutrition section.

SKIN, HAIR, AND NAILS

Your skin gets dry as you get older. Expect your dog to have skin problems, too. Over time, skin thickens, dries, and becomes less elastic. Your dog's hair may also lose its luster, becoming as brittle and dry as the "before" model in a shampoo commercial. The sebaceous glands, which secrete an oily, lubricating gel, may get plugged up and parch your dog's skin. Or these glands can go into overdrive, pumping out excessive amounts of waxy secretions and leading to a distinctly "doggy" smell.

Since an older dog's nails can become very brittle and grow at an alarming rate, pedicures will become less of a luxury and more a necessity as your dog ages. Dry, itchy skin can be irritating and cause your dog to scratch all night and all day. This can drive you crazy after a while. But, an even more important reason for treating these changes in the skin, hair, and nails is that left unattended, they can make your dog vulnerable to problems such as ingrown nails, eczema and fungal growths. Paying close attention to the condition of your dog's skin, hair, and nails will help you catch abcesses and infections in the earliest stages when they can be treated most easily. Regular grooming also helps you find and remove burrs and ticks.

BONES, JOINTS, AND MUSCLES

As dogs get older, their bones become thinner, more brittle, and more vulnerable to fracture. Older dogs also lose muscle mass and their joints stiffen. They aren't as powerful as they were when they were younger, and they may not be as comfortable sleeping on a hard floor. Many dogs break bones or develop joint troubles after injuries. A sensible approach to diet and exercise, taking your dog's age and physical condition into account, will help prevent breaks, strains and sprains and a soft, easy-access dog bed will comfort tired bones. Ask your veterinarian whether your older dog would benefit from calcium supplements or any other change in diet to help keep bones, muscles and joints strong. Massage is also a helpful way to soothe an achy body.

Arthritis can cause pain and inhibit movement. Some breeds are more prone to these problems than others, but arthritis is a serious problem for many older dogs. Vets often call it degenerative joint disease. While there is no way to reverse the problem at present, new veterinary drugs can ease pain and increase mobility.

BEHAVIORAL PROBLEMS

Is your older dog grouchy, nervous, or depressed? Changes in an older dog's behavior can arise from many conditions. For instance, a once-playful dog, suffering from the chronic pain of arthritis, may no longer be willing to tolerate young children cuddling with him. A dog who was the poster pet for obedience may now seem to be ignoring your commands because he can't hear you.

One serious canine condition that mimics Alzheimer's disease in humans is called cognitive dysfunction disorder. It can cause many different behavioral changes, including altered sleep cycles, emotional withdrawal, loss of appetite, tremors, urinating or defecating in the house, and compulsive behavior such as pacing or incessant barking for no apparent reason. There are drugs on the market to help ease the symptoms of cognitive dysfunction, but, at present, no reliable remedy exists to reverse the process.

METABOLISM

Your dog isn't moving as much as she once did. Instead of chasing cats, she's catching Zzzzs. It's the same equation we humans know only too well. Eat the same way you always did, exercise less and what do you gain? Weight. A healthy older dog wants to eat as much as she ever did. But decreasing activity while maintaining the same food intake quickly leads to obesity. In fact, veterinarians say that obesity is probably the most common problem they see in elderly dogs. Obesity can seriously aggravate heart disease, arthritis, and other coexisting conditions. Fortunately, most older dogs can get a handle on their weight problems by eating better and getting out more often. As dogs get older, their nutritional requirements change. We'll be getting into this subject in much more detail in the preventive care section of the book. Usually all it takes for a dog to get back the svelte shape she enjoyed in her youth is a different diet and sufficient exercise.

ELIMINATION

As time goes by, you may have to forgive an occasional accident. Your dog may not know he has to go until it's too late. When a dog gets older, his kidneys don't function as smoothly as they once did. Reduced kidney function can lead to excessive thirst—and you know what that leads to. The little puddles that appear in the corners of your kitchen or living room may remind you of the days when your dog was a pup. Digestive problems and decreased intestinal motility can also lead to diarrhea and flatulence. There are doggie diapers on the market today to help puppies and elderly dogs compensate for mistakes, but these aren't the only (or the best) solution.

If accidents occur only once in a while, taking your dog for more frequent walks could be all you need to do to solve the problem. Be sure your dog gets outside one more time before you go to bed at night. Nocturnal bedwetting is a particularly common problem. If troubles persist despite additional walks, your vet will be able to prescribe medicine to help your dog control his bowels and his bladder.

As this exhaustive list shows, lots of things change as our faithful companions age. The best way to face these changes is to educate yourself about the way your dog's body works. Take the preventive measures you need to ensure a happy old age for your beloved pet, and learn what your options are for treatment and management if your dog develops a health problem. Good health just doesn't happen. It's the direct result of your conscientious effort to take care of your pet.

PREVENTIVE CARE
AND FIRST AID

Besides scheduling regular visits to the vet, serving up healthy food and providing the opportunity for regular exercise are the two most important things you can do to increase your dog's chances of living to a ripe old age.

CHAPTER THREE

diet for an older dog

An ounce of prevention is worth a pound of cure. As surely as this old adage applies to your health, so it does to your older dog. On a daily basis, preventive health care means that you're careful about what you eat and that you make time for physical exercise. The same formula works for your dog. In fact, besides scheduling regular visits to the vet, serving up healthy food and providing the opportunity for regular exercise are the two most important things you can do to increase your dog's chances of living to a ripe old age. No matter what your dog's age, it's also a good idea to keep a first aid kit in your home and to make yourself familiar with the basics of veterinary first aid. Treating minor health problems effectively prevents them from developing into major illnesses. And knowing what to do in an emergency can save your dog's life.

Supermarket pet care aisles are bright and colorful places. The dog food section alone offers dozens of brands with brilliant labels and evocative names like Nature's Recipe, Trainer's Choice, and Mighty Champ. More and more products are being designed especially for older dogs. These are marketers' answers to our concern about our aging pets' health. The television commercials and magazine ads that promote these foods show healthy, happy dogs bounding across shiny kitchen floors to chow down. But they are not necessarily the answers pet owners need.

Appetizingly named and vividly labeled, the cans of wet food and bags of kibble we buy conjure up images of T-bone steaks and juicy roast chicken. The $11 billion pet food industry can well afford the marketing expertise necessary to make their products appealing to consumers. But who are they really selling to? Let's face it. Left to their natural urges, most dogs would eat just about anything. We're the ones pet food manufacturers are trying to impress, and we're the only ones who can judiciously choose the best, well-rounded diets for our canine friends.

WHAT'S REALLY IN THAT CAN OF DOG FOOD?

TV ads and pet food labels tell dog owners what they want to hear: that the food in those cans and bags is as wholesome and nutritious as mom's home cooking. Unfortunately, this isn't always true. Instead of the scrumptious meals owners envision when they serve up their dogs' dinners, what they may actually be plopping onto the plate can include hooves, feathers, and even diseased and cancerous animal parts. Needless to say, these are not the most nourishing ingredients. Some veterinarians believe that dogs who are fed such foods are at greater risk of developing cancer and other diseases.

The Association of American Feed Control Officials (AAFCO) and the Pet Food Institute, an industry trade group, agree that diseased animal parts should not be part of a dog's diet. But, while many dog food manufacturers do comply with AAFCO quality guidelines, some do not. And the real problem is that AAFCO standards aren't all that high. AAFCO's minimal

nutrient standards for dogs allow pet food manufacturers to use animal by-products in their foods. By-products are the parts of slaughtered animals that are not considered fit for human consumption. They include bones, blood, intestines, lungs, ligaments, and almost any other part of the animal left on the slaughterhouse floor.

The federal Food and Drug Administration (FDA) Center for Veterinary Medicine doesn't regulate the manufacture of pet food, but it has established labeling standards. FDA standards require dog food manufacturers to properly identify their products, to make an accurate net quantity statement on the label, to list ingredients in order of weight, and to post the manufacturer's address on the label (in case consumers want to complain). The consumer's best bet, therefore, is to read labels. Just as you note what kinds of ingredients are contained in the foods you buy for you and your family, take the time to look at the ingredients listed on dog food labels.

READING THE FINE PRINT

As a general rule, the more you pay for dog food, the better quality product you'll get. But a premium price isn't always a guarantee that food is fresh and nutritious. The pet food industry readily acknowledges the use of by-products in pet foods, but AAFCO requires dog food manufacturers to meet certain nutritional standards before using particular language on the label.

Manufacturers must list ingredients by weight, from highest to lowest weight, the same way that packaged foods for humans are listed. One trick manufacturers use to get around this AAFCO requirement is called "splitting." Ingredients may be listed in order of weight, but components of more inexpensive ingredients are listed separately. For example, a can of dog food may list the top ingredients as chicken, ground yellow corn, ground wheat, and

corn gluten meal. This listing makes it look as though chicken is the primary ingredient of the dog food. In fact, ground yellow corn and corn gluten meal are really both components of corn meal. Add their weights together and corn meal is the primary ingredient!

You may be impressed by claims such as "all natural," "healthy," or "light" on dog food label—but don't be fooled. Neither the AAFCO nor the FDA regulates such claims. They can mean whatever manufacturers want them to mean.

Nutritional values are also set by weight—by dry weight. Canned dog food generally contains 75 percent moisture, while dry food contains only 10 percent. So, to find out how much protein is in a can of dog food, you must multiply the amount listed on the label by four. To get the same information about dry food, multiply the amount on the label by 1.1. These formulas are specified by AAFCO.

The industry uses special terms to signal how much nutritional protein is in pet food. For instance, when the label reads "Dr. X's Chicken Dog Food," this means the can must contain 95 percent chicken. "Dr. X's Chicken Dinner," on the other hand, need only contain 25 percent chicken. Any dog food labeled a "dinner," "platter," or the like needs to contain only 25 percent of the meat advertised. If the label reads "Dr. X's Chicken and Bacon Dinner," the chicken and bacon together must make up 25 percent of the food's dry weight, with a minimum of 3 percent dry weight from each ingredient. This can might contain 22 percent bacon and only 3 percent chicken, the more expensive ingredient. When you see the word "flavor" on a label, it means that a substance other than meat, poultry, or fish has been used to give the food the flavor of meat, poultry, or fish. These products don't have to contain any real meat, poultry, or fish at all.

Shopping Guide

The Animal Protection Institute (API) recommends that consumers follow this advice when shopping for dog food in pet stores or supermarkets:

❧ Make sure the label has the AAFCO guarantee.

❧ Stay away from meat and bone meals, by-products, and by-product meals.

❧ Look for meat as the first ingredient.

❧ Consider which grains are in the formula—rice is the most digestible of all grains used in pet foods.

❧ If corn is listed more than once in the first five ingredients, try another brand.

❧ Look for foods that use natural preservatives such as mixed tocopherols or vitamins C and E rather than chemical preservatives like ethoxyquin, BHT and BHA.

❧ Check the expiration data to ensure freshness.

❧ When you open a bag of food, be sure to smell it. If it smells at all rancid, return it to the store you purchased it from for exchange or refund.

❧ When changing foods, mix ⅓ of the new food to ⅔ of the old food and increase the new food a little every day to prevent gastric upset.

❧ Take note of your dog's stool when changing pet foods. It should be firm but not hard and have minimal odor.

❧ Note your dog's coat and weight to ensure the new food suits individual needs and does not cause major weight loss or gain.

❧ Stay away from trendy foods that make unverifiable claims related to animal health.

❧ When storing pet food, keep it in a sealed container in a cool dry place.

❧ Always be sure that in addition to proper nutrition you supply your dog with fresh water at all times as well as adequate exercise and lots of love.

(Reprinted with permission of the Animal Protection Institute)

Diet-Related Diseases

DISEASE	DIETARY RISK FACTORS
Obesity	Overfeeding of foods high in fats and calories
Kidney Disease	Toxins in foods, dehydration
Bladder Stones	Dehydration, poor quality diet
Heart Failure	High sodium diet
Diabetes	Diet high in fats and low in fiber, too many sweet treats

When you're looking for the best food for your dog, the amount of meat in the product is not the only—or even the most important—consideration. In fact, an all-meat diet is far from well-balanced. Dogs need vegetables and grains, too. Wheat, soy, corn, peanut hulls, and vegetable proteins are a significant part of most dog food formulas today. What matters most is how digestible these grains are. The moldy old grains and meat by-products used in inferior products are not easily digestible. In the short term, they can cause diarrhea, gas, and vomiting. Feeding dogs inferior quality foods may contribute to the development of disease in the long run.

Preservatives must be listed on dog food labels, too, and this is important information because some preservatives—butylated hydroxyanisole (BHA), butylated hydroxytoluene (BHT), and ethoxyquin—can be harmful to dogs' health if consumed on a long-term basis. These preservatives, most frequently used in bags of kibble to extend shelf life, are suspected carcinogens.

Although there has not been sufficient research to prove the connection between these preservatives and the development of cancer in dogs, the FDA was concerned enough in 1997 to ask pet food manufacturers to voluntarily reduce the amount of ethoxyquin used in their products by half. Some manufacturers responded to the FDA's request and to consumers' concerns by switching to more natural preservatives such as Vitamin C (ascorbate), Vitamin E (mixed tocopherols), and oils of rosemary, clove, or other spices.

Dozens of other substances are added to dog food, including texturizers, lubricants, non-nutrient sweeteners, flavor enhancers, emulsifiers, and artificial color. Manufacturers must ensure that these additives are not toxic; however, they are not required to test for possible toxic interactions among these ingredients.

How do pet food manufacturers justify claims they make on the label that the food they produce provides the nutrients dogs need? Although it is no longer required, the more reputable pet food companies still base nutrient values on feeding trials that last six months or more. The food is considered nutritionally balanced if test dogs maintain weight and health while being fed the product over a six-month period.

In real life, however, dogs consume these products for ten to fifteen years. Feed tests can't predict long-term

nutritional value. Smaller companies limit testing to palatability studies, which are even less informative. They simply present a new recipe for pet food to test dogs while a control group is fed the current recipe. Testers weigh the volume of food consumed by dogs in each group. Most dog food manufacturers use palatability tests to be sure their new products will be appealing to dogs, but palatability tests provide no information about how nourishing a food is.

SPECIAL DIETS FOR OLDER DOGS

Dogs' nutritional needs aren't that different from humans', and, like ours, they can change as the years go by. Just like older people, older dogs usually need fewer calories per pound of body weight than they did when they were young. Let an old dog eat too much and he's sure to gain weight. Many older dogs need less fat in their diets as their ability to digest fat decreases. But at the same time, older dogs digest and process nutrients less efficiently. They often need more nutritious food or food supplements to satisfy their vitamin and mineral requirements.

THE MOST IMPORTANT VITAMINS AND NUTRIENTS FOR OLDER DOGS

Whether your dog is supermodel-slender or pleasingly plump, she will begin to need food that's easier to digest as she moves into her later years. A good diet for your older dog will contain high-quality protein, fats, and carbohydrates. Good senior diets also contain enough fiber to ensure regularity. Look for low-salt formulas with vitamins A and E added. Studies show that these antioxidant vitamins may help to slow down the aging process. Many veterinarians recommend premium (also called natural) pet foods for older dogs. Ask your vet for suggestions. Premium pet foods, such as Science Diet and Hill's Prescription Diet, are usually sold in veterinarians' offices.

Increasingly, premium brands are also available in pet superstores and even in supermarkets.

All a healthy older dog may need to keep that spring in her step is a switch to one of the many premium (or natural) foods specifically designed for elderly pets. For smaller, frailer dogs, geriatric formulas provide more dense caloric energy, easier digestibility, better flavor, and more nutrition. Formulas designed for older dogs with a tendency to put on weight are still nutritionally enhanced, but lack the extra calories and may have a blander taste to discourage overeating.

OBESITY IN OLDER DOGS

Obesity is not just an aesthetic issue in dogs. It is a serious health problem that shortens a dog's life span. Overweight dogs are more likely to suffer from diabetes, heart disease, and arthritis. They often develop breathing problems. Obesity also contributes to liver disease, hypertension, constipation, heat intolerance, and increases risks if your dog goes under anesthesia. Obesity can occur at any stage of a dog's life, but it is most likely to creep up on an older dog whose metabolism has slowed down. What can you do to help your dog slim down?

First, talk to your veterinarian. Although the usual cause of obesity is overeating and lack of exercise, some diseases can cause dogs to pack on the pounds so you want to be sure that your pet is in good health before you reach for the diet books. Once your dog has a clean bill of health, there are two ways to proceed.

You can start simply feeding the dog less. Veterinarians generally recommend that a dog's calorie intake be cut back by a quarter each week for two weeks. Weigh the dog at the beginning of the diet and then on a weekly basis. To weigh a smaller dog, simply pick her up and step

How Does Your Dog Measure Up?

Underweight	Her ribs are visible with minimal fat cover. Bony prominences (hips, shoulders) are easily felt with minimal overlying fat. There is a marked abdominal tuck when she is viewed from the side and a marked hourglass shape when viewed from above.
Ideal	Her ribs are easily palpable with a slight fat cover. Bony prominences can be felt through a small amount of overlying fat. There is an abdominal tuck when she is viewed from the side and a well-proportioned waist when viewed from above.
Overweight	Her ribs are difficult to feel because the fat cover is thicker but the bony structure can still be felt. Bony prominences are covered by a moderate layer of fat. There is little or no abdominal tuck or waist when she is viewed from the side and her back is slightly broadened when viewed from above. A slight pot belly, or rounding of the abdomen, is present.
Obese	Her ribs are difficult to feel because of the thick covering of fat. Bony prominences are also covered by a moderate to thick layer of fat. There is a pendulous bulge in her tummy and no waist when she is viewed from the side. Her back is markedly broadened when viewed from above. Fat deposits can also be found on her face and limbs.

on the bathroom scale while holding her in your arms; deduct your own weight from the total to determine your dog's weight. Larger dogs will have to go into the vet's office for weigh-ins.

You can also switch to a prescription diet dog food. Ask your veterinarian to recommend a brand. These foods are specifically formulated to contain the nutrients your dog needs while dieting. They are also a bit less tasty than regular fare to discourage overeating. Read the label to find out how much you should be serving at each meal.

Another way to help your dog slim down is to stop feeding table scraps. Dogs who beg at the supper table are usually rewarded with fattening morsels such as fat trimmed from the meat on your plate. Dog biscuits and other treats are also high in calories; offer praise or extra affection as an alternative to treats. Increasing the amount of exercise your dog gets is a crucial part of weight-loss success. Add an extra walk each day, or increase the length of the walks you regularly take. Encourage your dog to run and jump. You'll reap the health benefits of the extra exercise, too.

NUTRACEUTICALS—FOODS THAT HEAL

The notion that foods can heal is as old as the earth itself. Medical historians say that early humans watched animals seek out particular plants when they weren't feeling well and learned about healing herbs that way. Today, when pet foods come out of cans and packages, the roles are reversed. Humans must help their animal companions return to natural healing.

Can eating cabbage boost a dog's immunity? Does garlic reduce the risk of heart disease? Scientists have isolated hundreds of "nutraceuticals," non-nutrient substances found in plants. Although research is still in the early stages, scientists believe that nutraceuticals may be the reason that people whose diets are rich in fruits and vegetables tend to live longer. But does this research apply to dogs? Many veterinarians think so. The following are some of the most promising nutraceuticals for canines.

Garlic: Garlic fights colds, lowers cholesterol, and may prevent heart disease. Repeated studies show that allicin, a substance found in garlic, lowers cholesterol. Try making a garlic condiment for you dog by soaking raw cloves in tamari soy sauce mixed with a little water. Add half a teaspoon of the soaked garlic to your dog's food. (Heaping helpings of garlic will give your dog bad breath and, more seriously, may cause problems with red blood cells. Serve up small doses and check with your veterinarian if you have specific concerns.)

Co-enzyme Q-10: Available in many premium dog foods and in supplement form, this substance helps prevent gum disease.

Indoles: Indoles, compounds found in all cruciferous vegetables, boost immune functioning in animal studies. Grind up a little cooked cabbage in a food processor and add it to your dog's dish. Steam broccoli and serve it with butter or garlic soaked in tamari.

Perna Canaliculus (green-lipped) mussel: Contains glycosamines and chondroitin sulfate, substances shown to ease arthritis pain and to help build up connective tissue.

Can be found in supplements available at natural food stores and pet supermarkets.

Antioxidants: Vitamin C can be given as a supplement or found in oranges provided as whole foods, if your dog likes them. Vitamin E, a natural moisturizer, can help restore luster to skin, coat, and nails. Look for vitamin C and vitamin E in premium food formulas.

HOW MUCH FOOD DOES YOUR DOG NEED?

A thirty-pound dog requires about thirty calories per pound of body weight per day. Large breeds generally require less (about twenty calories per pound per day) and small breeds require more (about forty calories per pound per day). In general, older dogs require fewer calories per pound of body weight than they did when they were young. In winter, dogs who go outside a lot will need more calories. When the weather is very hot, dogs may want to eat less but they will need the same amount of calories. Ask your veterinarian about supplementing meals with high-quality snacks or switching to a more energy-dense food during the summer. Of course, each dog has his own idiosyncratic requirements. Keep an eye on your dog. Is he overweight? Underweight? Energetic? Lethargic? The way your dog shapes up is the best clue to whether he's getting enough to eat.

DO-IT-YOURSELF DOG FOOD

The pet food industry has not always produced enough products to fill entire aisles of supermarket shelves. Before the 1950s, when post-war leisure and affluence combined to create new markets for pet food manufacturers, people simply fed their dogs bones and table scraps. Such a haphazard diet, of course, is far from balanced or nutritionally complete and we're not recommending that you feed your dog a homemade diet based on scraps and leftovers. But, it is true that many commercial dog foods contain preservatives, additives, and inferior-grade ingredients. If you are concerned about your older dog's ability to digest and absorb the nutrients he needs, you might want to consider switching to a homemade diet.

Make any change in your dog's diet gradually. A sudden switch from an older dog's usual fare can cause gastrointestinal upset. Introduce new foods slowly, and one at a time, to be sure that you'll notice food allergies. To begin, you may simply want to supplement your older dog's commercial-food diet with homemade meals two or three times a week. A balanced homemade meal should contain plenty of protein: boneless chicken, lean beef, cottage cheese, and hard-boiled eggs are good sources. Pureed vegetables, such as carrots, peas, green beans, parsnips, or squash, help deliver other nutrients your dog needs. Dogs also require a certain amount of fat for energy.

As you can see, it isn't always simple to be sure that your dog is getting a balanced diet when you feed her from scratch. Some veterinarians are also concerned that foods we know are healthy for humans aren't always healthy for canines. Garlic and onions, for instance, may or may not be an appropriate part of your dog's diet. To be on the safe side, before altering your dog's diet in any significant way, please consult with your veterinarian.

A HOLISTIC VIEW

Many holistic veterinarians recommend feeding dogs raw meat. They believe that cooking robs meat of important nutrients and point out that a raw food diet more closely resembles the way animals naturally eat in the wild. Some research does support claims that dogs and cats achieve a higher level of health—glossier coats, stronger teeth and skeletal structure—when they are fed a raw diet. Holistic veterinarians also point out that dogs' digestive systems are stronger than humans'. They believe that dogs' diges-

---

Serve Your Dog Right

Most people simply put their dog's food and water bowls on the floor. But, for a large older dog, this arrangement may not work. Dogs with stiff joints can find bending down to eat a painful process. Pet supply stores and catalogs sell specially-designed tables with cutouts for water and food bowls. They come in various heights to suit a wide variety of dogs.

---

tive juices contain more than enough hydrochloric acid to kill off any harmful bacteria in uncooked meat. But hazards could still remain. New strains of E. coli and salmonella could cause problems, especially in older dogs whose systems are more fragile. Giving dogs raw bones to chew also tempts fate. Bones, especially lighter ones like chicken bones, can splinter and become lodged in a dog's throat. Again, before you make any important changes in your dog's diet, talk to your veterinarian. For resources on diet and nutrition, see the appendices at the end of this book. There are also many excellent books devoted to pets' nutritional needs. These include:

Martin, Ann N. *Foods Pets Die For: Shocking Facts about Pet Food.* New Sage Press, 1997.

Pitcairn, DVM, Richard H. *Dr. Pitcairn's Complete Guide to Natural Health for Dogs and Cats.* Rodale Press, 1997.

Puotinen, C.J. *The Encyclopedia of Natural Pet Care.* Keats Publishing, 1998

Schulze, Kymthy. *Natural Nutrition for Dogs and Cats: The Ultimate Pet Diet.* Hay House, 1999.

CHAPTER FOUR

exercise to keep your dog agile

Daily exercise routines will not only keep your dog trim and flexible, but will also help prevent age-related health problems. Veterinarians generally recommend two daily exercise sessions, each lasting fifteen to twenty minutes. Of course, you'll want to tailor the workouts to the particular needs and predilections of your older dog. Some dogs love Frisbees while others live to chase tennis balls. There are swimmers and jumpers and obstacle course runners. But we haven't met a dog yet who doesn't thoroughly enjoy a good, brisk walk in the park. Just getting outside in the fresh air, sniffing the ground, and stopping to socialize with other dogs is many dogs' idea of heaven. Coincidentally, it's one of the best things a loving human can do with his canine companion.

Regular exercise is as important for your dog as it is for you. Aren't you glad you can share in the process? Regular exercise will keep your dog's weight in line, strengthen his heart and lungs, increase his stamina, alertness, and energy. Exercise also strengthens your dog's muscles and bones and keeps his joints limber. Dogs who are exercised regularly won't become restless and bored as sedentary dogs do. Dogs who get enough exercise are less likely to develop behavioral problems such as digging, barking, and chewing your favorite slippers. Last but not least, exercise makes your dog happy. By triggering the release of brain chemicals called endorphins, aerobic exercise, such as running and jumping, lifts mood and enhances well-being.

HOW MUCH EXERCISE DOES YOUR OLDER DOG NEED?

Because older dogs are generally slowing down, their fitness routines may need fine-tuning. The amount and type of exercise that best suits your dog depends on a variety of factors, including age, breed, and general health. Although veterinarians suggest two fifteen-to-twenty-minute workouts each day, there is no absolute rule about exercise for dogs. The most important thing is to be consistent: create a routine and stick with it. Regular exercise builds strength and flexibility. Your dog will also come to depend on his exercise routine, to look forward and enjoy the time spent having fun with you.

Despite your best intentions, you may find that a busy work schedule and hectic family life keep you from taking your dog on his daily rounds. An older dog who doesn't get enough exercise won't complain as vociferously as a younger pup will. He may just roll over and take a longer nap. You can't rely on your faithful companion to let you know that it's time for a walk; the responsibility for creating and maintaining an exercise routine is yours. To keep your dog interested—and to preserve your own enthusiasm—make sure that the daily dose of exercise isn't just a chore. Make it fun.

Regular exercise pays off in many ways. Studies show that moderate exercise helps older dogs stay trim and is a major factor in the prevention of a variety of age-related illnesses, including heart disease, arthritis,

gastrointestinal disease, and respiratory problems. Dogs who get enough exercise are happier and better behaved. Older dogs who have trouble sleeping through the night will rest easier when they get enough exercise.

As your dog grows older, you may want to gradually reduce the length of daily workouts or change the kind of exercise he gets. A dog who ran with you in earlier years may want to slow it down to a jog now. A dog who jumped after Frisbees all afternoon may be content to fetch a few tennis balls. When you take your dog for his annual check-up, ask your veterinarian what kind of exercise schedule is optimal for him at his age and in his unique health condition. Skip vigorous workout sessions on extremely hot summer days and guard against slips and falls in winter weather. Taking a few sensible precautions can keep your older dog happy and fit, willing and able to enjoy the benefits of exercise throughout his life.

WORKOUT BASICS

When you design an exercise program for yourself, whether you visit the local gym or go for a run around the neighborhood, you are careful to include the elements you need for all-around fitness. You start out slowly with warm-up exercises, make sure that you get a good cardio-vascular workout, add in some strength training, and finish with a cool-down routine that gently stretches the muscles you have worked. Pay the same kind of attention to your dog's exercise routine.

Older dogs especially need a gentle warm-up period at the beginning of every exercise session. Before you take your dog out for a run, spend a few minutes bending and stretching her limbs. Find a comfortable sitting or kneeling position, hold your dog, and gently stretch her legs, one at a time. Make a game of it. Talk to her, praising her strong and beautiful limbs, while you help with these easy

stretches. Encourage your dog's natural urges to arch and bend her spine—the "dog stretches" that humans emulate in yoga positions and warm-ups for calisthenics—and praise her whenever she stretches her spine this way. It's a wonderful way to stay limber and a great way to begin a workout.

Once you and your dog are warmed up, start walking at a moderate pace. Pay attention to your dog's natural instincts. She may want to walk slowly for the full fifteen minutes one day. Another day, feeling much perkier, she may want you to chase her or throw the ball a few times. Follow her lead to keep things interesting. No matter how you reach it, the goal is to keep your older dog moving at a reasonably brisk pace for ten to fifteen minutes. Always include warm up and cool down periods at the beginning and end of each exercise sessions, even on slow days when your dog is doing more walking than running. The entire exercise period, including warm up and cool down, should add up to fifteen to twenty minutes.

Vary the pace with a few short sprints if your dog enjoys them, or take a route that includes a hill or two to help build up strength and endurance. Encourage a dog who is reluctant to run by standing off at a reasonable distance and calling her to you. If you have a friend or partner who works out with you, make a game of calling the dog to run back and forth between the two of you. Reward your dog with praise and a healthy treat for participating on days when she's feeling sluggish. Whatever you do, the benefits of walking, jogging, or running can't be beat. Your dog's heart, lungs, and circulatory system are getting a solid workout.

Don't forget to cool down at the end of an exercise session. Slow the pace for a few minutes. Stop and stretch. Spend a little time sitting in the sun or in the cool shade

of a tree, if your schedule permits. Let your dog enjoy the sensuous pleasures of being outdoors—the sights, smells, and other sensations—so she'll be eager to jump on the leash for the next time.

EXERCISE FOR FUN AND FITNESS

If your older dog is getting bored with his regular workout routine, keep him in great shape by making exercise sessions more fun. You are starting out with a major advantage: your dog likes nothing more than your attention and exercise sessions mean spending time with you. A little variation in the routine can add more excitement. You don't want to confuse your dog by putting so much variety into the workout sessions that he doesn't know what to expect! Not unlike people, dogs prefer their lives to be fairly predictable. But they do get bored. Use a little creativity to keep your dog interested and you'll take the work out of your dog's workout.

What your dog likes to do for exercise depends, in part, on his size and breed. If your dog is a mixed breed, consider the parts of the mix. What were your dog's ancestors doing? If he's a Newfoundland, they were probably swimming. If he's a corgi, they were herding. If he's a Labrador retriever, they were hunting. Use what you know about your dog's ancestry to challenge his natural skills and add spice to his life. Almost every dog enjoys walking, running, and playing games such as catch or tag, so you can start with those activities as a basis for the workout routine. Think of yourself as your dog's personal trainer and add other activities to keep him mentally and physically challenged. Here are a few ideas to get your started.

EXERCISE BY SIZE AND BREED

A sporting dog, such as a spaniel or a retriever, will enjoy any and all fetching activities. A quick dip in the water, if weather permits and you live in an area where that's an option, can add zest.

Working dogs, such as rottweilers and huskies, relish a challenge. Their ancestors spent plenty of time engaged in strenuous activity. Focus on exercise that uses lots of energy and helps maintain stamina. These dogs need plenty of time outside, running and playing, even in their golden years.

Toy breeds, such as Pekingese and Chihuahas, are not so athletic. They prefer sitting on your lap and cuddling to long, demanding runs. That doesn't mean these dogs aren't peppy and fun loving, however. They love to play with chew toys and balls, indoors as well as outdoors.

Hounds, such as beagles and bassets, love to chase things. Their ancestors specialized in tracking down prey. These dogs love to run and they can overdo it, especially as they get older. It's very important to help these dogs warm up before workouts and cool down afterwards. Give hounds an opportunity to stretch in an enclosed yard or other enclosed area.

Terriers, such as Jack Russells and West Highlands, are born to fetch. Rather than run by your side as you jog, these fun-loving dogs prefer frolicking. They will play Frisbee for as long as you (or your children) can stand it. Larger terriers, of course, need more exercise than smaller terriers. But, large, small, or medium, they all need to be reminded to slow down. Older terriers can get winded before they're ready to stop roughhousing. Keep that in mind and limit vigorous workout sessions to ten or fifteen minutes.

Non-sporting dogs are a varied bunch. The larger ones, such as poodles and dalmations, can take as much

exercise as any other large dog. But smaller non-sporting dogs, such as the Bichon Frise and the Lhasa Apso, don't need—or want—such a strenuous workout. These dogs enjoy quiet walks in the park and indoor play, particularly as they age.

Herding dogs, such as shepherds and collies, are all-around athletes. They enjoy long walks and, even as they age, often have enough stamina for twenty-to-thirty-minute runs. They're good at playing catch. They like to swim, too. And, especially in their later years, their com-

bination of energy and tolerant personality makes them wonderful companions for children.

DON'T OVERDO IT

Your older dog wants to please you. That's a wonderful trait but it can get her in trouble when she thinks you want her to run and jump and play catch beyond the point that it's comfortable and fun. Keep close tabs on your dog during exercise sessions and play times. Does she seem tired? Is she breathing hard? Are her sides heaving? At the first sign of any discomfort, stop exercising, let your dog have a short drink of water, and allow her to relax. There's no practical way for dog owners to monitor heart rate—all that's really necessary is observation. Be sure your dog isn't puffing or panting.

Their beautiful fur coats keep dogs warm in the winter, but they can make them vulnerable to heatstroke in the summer. In very warm weather, keep your dog indoors at midday. When the weather's hot, city pavement gets hot, too. You won't feel the heat through your shoes, but your dog could burn the pads of her feet. Schedule exercise times early in the morning, at dusk, or in the evening. The sun won't be as hot at these times and the sidewalks will be cooler.

Winter also has its hazards. Smaller, short-haired dogs in particular need to wear sweaters when they go out to exercise during the winter months. As your dog gets older, she may become more sensitive to cold weather. If she does, keep her indoors on the coldest days and shorten walks from twenty minutes to ten minutes on days that are medium-cold. Watch out for your dog's feet in winter, too: the chemicals used to melt snow and ice can burn the pads of her feet. Try to keep her from walking in areas where road salt or road sand has been used. Staying outside too long in cold weather isn't any wiser for dogs than it is for humans. Dogs can get frostbite and their feet can get chapped, just as our hands do. If you notice any tiny cuts or cracks in the pads of your dog's feet, coat them with petroleum jelly to soothe discomfort. If the trouble persists, consult your veterinarian.

EXERCISE ALTERNATIVES

AGILITY TRAINING

Agility trials, timed events in which dogs compete while moving through obstacle courses, are gaining popularity, but most people with older dogs don't think their pets are ready for this kind of organized event. Well, think again. The latest twist on agility training is agility just for fun. People are getting together at local parks to set up tunnels, bar jumps, and weave poles. They coach their dogs through these casual courses, alone or with others. It's an alternate to the usual walk or run and the socializing adds to the fun. The bars are lowered for older dogs and dogs are generally allowed to take the course as they please, choosing to participate only in the activities they wish. To find out more about agility training or to find a play group in your area, start with the Just for Fun Agility Web site at www.dog-play.com/agility.

DOG PARKS

Is your dog a social animal? Are you? Then off-leash dog parks where dogs are free to run and play with other dogs could be your dream come true. These dog parks, organized and maintained by loose collaborations of dog lovers, are increasingly popular, particularly in urban areas where leash laws restrict dogs' freedom in most places. Ten years ago, there were only about twenty officially sanctioned dog parks in the United States. Now there are about 350 and more are opening all the time. These special parks, which often provide fresh, clean water and pooper-scooper bags, are usually fenced for safety. Within park limits, dogs can be as rowdy as they want to be. That's what's great—and also what can be dangerous—about dog parks. When you take a dog, especially a younger or older dog, to a dog park, you need to pay close attention to your pet at all times. Watch carefully when she approaches, or is approached, by another canine. Is the interaction friendly? Aggressive dogs don't really belong in dog parks, but from time to time they do visit. And, some dogs may interpret very friendly behavior as aggression and become frightened. But if your dog enjoys running with the pack or chasing a few balls with a couple of friends, the dog park is probably her kind of place. For more information, visit the Web site: www.Dogpark.com.

CHAPTER FIVE

first aid

No matter how hard we try to take the best possible care of our canine companions, accidents do happen. Also, as dogs age, they become more susceptible to little aches and pains. A younger dog will take a bruise or sting in stride, but for an older dog, these become a more serious matter. Make your dog's life more comfortable by learning first aid and knowing how to provide simple home care for common minor ailments.

A FIRST AID PRIMER

No one likes to anticipate trouble, but being prepared is more than the boy scout motto—it can mean the difference between life and death. It's always best to consult your veterinarian whenever an accident or injury occurs, but there are times when immediate action is required. Following are first aid treatments for some of the most common accidents and injuries dogs experience.

HANDLING AN INJURED DOG

Injuries stir up adrenaline and can put even the most mild-mannered dog into a ferocious mood. You must be very careful about handling an injured dog, especially one that has been in a fight. Pain and fear can cause him to lash out, even at you. Before you begin any emergency treatment, muzzle the dog. You can create a makeshift muzzle with a length of gauze, a necktie, or a pair of pantyhose. A piece of rope will also work but it's less flexible and won't be as comfortable for the dog. Make a noose by tying a loose knot in the middle of the strip of material, leaving a large loop. Approach the dog quietly from behind, to avoid getting injured yourself, and slip the noose over your dog's snout. Quickly but gently, pull the noose taut about halfway up his nose. Wrap the gauze, necktie, pantyhose, or rope around your dog's muzzle several times, then pull the ends back and tie them behind his ears. If your dog is very small, you can accomplish the same purpose by simply wrapping a towel around his head. Whether you use a muzzle or a towel wrap, be sure that you leave the dog's nostrils uncovered so that he can breathe easily.

MOVING AN INJURED DOG

If your dog has been injured in a car accident or another trauma, he may have broken bones or internal injuries that you can't see. You want to move him as little as possible to avoid making matters worse. Try to immobilize your dog before moving him to your car to take the trip to the veterinarian's office. A board or a piece of cardboard large enough to support your dog works well as a supporting structure. A child's sled will also do. Move the dog, as smoothly and swiftly as possible, onto the flat surface. Then, restrain him there. Wrapping a sheet around the dog and tying it firmly to keep him still is an effective method. A smaller dog could be placed gently into a cardboard box with towels or sheets wedged around him to keep him from moving. Help your dog stay calm by talking to him in a soft, nurturing voice while you're preparing him for the trip.

FIGHTS, CUTS, AND BITES

Your dog may have the sweetest temperament in the world but he can still get into a tussle with another neighborhood dog. Fights frequently result in cuts and bites. If you find your dog in a clinch with another dog, be very careful about how you separate them. Don't jump into the fray. Dousing them with a bucket of cold water or spraying them with a garden hose is a much safer way to

intervene. Once the dogs are separated, give your dog a moment to calm down before you touch him. Talk to him in a quiet, comforting voice and approach him gently. (See Handling an Injured Dog on page 54)

First, check to see whether the skin is broken anywhere. When a dog has been in a fight, you're most likely to find cuts and bites around the neck, face, ears, and chest. Teeth bites that seem small and clean on the surface can be more serious than they look. Tissue under the skin may be damaged, too. The first thing to do is wipe all the blood from the surface so you can see what's really happening.

Using blunt-tipped scissors, clip the hair away from the wound. Dampen a face cloth or sponge with warm water and a mild disinfectant. Then, spread a layer of petroleum jelly around the site of the wound to keep the wound clean. Now that you can see the injury better, you will know whether the dog needs veterinary attention. You can

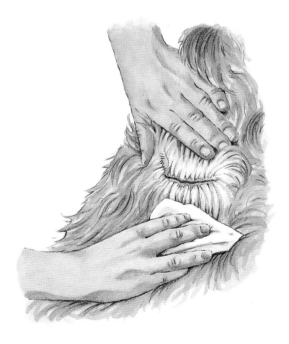

treat minor lacerations (scrapes and surface cuts) your-self, using an antiseptic cream and taping a light layer of gauze over the injury. But don't try to treat deep cuts on your own—get the dog to the veterinarian right away—for professional medical treatment.

BROKEN LIMBS

Don't overestimate your expertise in a situation like this. If your dog has a broken limb, the most important thing you can do is get him to a veterinarian. To do so, you'll need to immobilize the limb so that your dog can be trans-ported as comfortably as possible.

The first thing you need to ascertain is what kind of fracture your dog has. Your dog won't be much help to you in weighing the severity of the situation. There are two kinds of fractures—simple and compound. A simple fracture is one that doesn't break through the skin, while a compound fracture does. The area will probably be bloody and it is susceptible to infection. Compound fractures are emergencies that require an immediate trip to the vet. While a simple fracture isn't as serious, treatment should not be postponed longer than necessary.

With a simple fracture, you may not even know right away that anything is wrong. Dogs are notoriously stoic. Although he may not whimper or whine, your dog will undoubtedly favor a broken limb—if he can walk on it at all. There are other telltale clues. A limb that looks differ-ent from the others, one that has a lump in it or a paw that is twisted in the wrong direction are all signs that something isn't right.

A simple fracture may not cause your dog a lot of pain. In that case, you may be able to load him into the car for the trip to the vet without splinting the injured leg. To keep the dog comfortable, hold him in your lap or sit near him in the car. Pet him and talk to him in a gentle, reassuring voice on your way to the veterinary hospital. In the case of a compound fracture or a simple fracture that is more painful, you will need to immobi-lize the limb.

If the break is below the knee, you can apply a splint. To make a simple splint, roll several sheets of newspa-per or a magazine around the area. Depending on the size of your dog, you can use a popsicle stick, tongue depressor, or a yardstick to immobilize the limb. Break off the yardstick to the length you need and cover both sharp ends with masking tape to avoid further injury. Make sure the splint extends above the knee and below the paw. Cover the splint with gauze or a bath towel, if you wish, and secure it with band-age tape.

Don't try to splint a break above the knee. You can do more damage than good by pulling at the area. Instead of splinting the limb, immobilize the dog. A large or medium sized dog can be immobilized on a piece of plywood board or a sturdy piece of card-board. You could also use a child's sled. For a smaller dog, a tea tray, a broiling pan, or a smaller piece of wood will do. Place the dog on the flat surface, or slip it under him. First, tape the broken limb in place, with bandage tape, and then immobilize the dog's whole body, using large pieces of tape to connect him loosely to the flat surface. Don't try to clean the wound or remove foreign objects such as glass, wood fragments, or dirt. Leave a delicate job like this to the veterinarian who can do the work when the dog is under anesthesia.

CHOKING

Unfortunately, dogs are compelled to put just about anything in their mouths, but not everything goes down easily. Dogs can choke on toys and large pieces of food, but splintered bones and twigs are more likely to get lodged in a dog's throat. To prevent accidents, never give your dog any kind of small bones to chew as treats and don't let your dog play with toys small enough to be swallowed.

When your dog is choking, the first thing to do is find out whether what he's choking on can be pulled out of his mouth. Twigs and bones can get stuck between a dog's teeth, or at the back of the throat. Get someone to hold your dog gently while you open his mouth and look down his throat. Using a pair of blunt-edged tweezers or a pair of pliers, carefully remove the foreign object. Try to keep your fingers out of the dog's mouth so that you don't get bitten.

When you can't reach the foreign body this way, the next step is to lift your dog into the air and hold him upside down to try and dislodge the foreign object. If your dog's too heavy to lift all the way off the ground, just lift his back legs in the air. Either way, put your arms under the dog's belly and slide them back until they catch him at the groin, just in front of the hind legs. Give the dog a gentle shake to dislodge what's choking him.

Sometimes, an object that's choking a dog has moved
so far down the windpipe that shaking doesn't dislodge
it. Then it's time for the Heimlich maneuver. The
moves are basically the same for dogs as they are
for people. For large dogs, wrap your arms around
the belly, just under the rib cage. With smaller dogs,
you can use your hands instead of your arms. Press
down forcefully two or three times. If this procedure
doesn't dislodge the object, take the dog to the veterinarian immediately.

Be Prepared

The best thing you can do to help your dog in an emergency is to be prepared in advance. Here are some steps to take so you're always ready:

❧ Add your veterinarian's number to your list of emergency phone numbers and keep it right by your phone.

❧ On your next visit, ask the veterinarian if there is an emergency vet center in your area so you know where to take your dog if your own vet isn't available. And, to make sure you know the fastest way to get there, take a rehearsal drive.

❧ Keep the National Animal Poison Control Center's 24-hour credit card hotline on hand (800-548-2423). Specialists here are trained to listen to your dog's symptoms and give you advice on what to do if you think your dog has ingested poison. There is a $30 consultation fee for this service that includes follow-up consultations with your veterinarian.

❧ Have a first-aid kit on hand.

POISONING

Again, because dogs are omnivores who see just about everything as something to eat, poisoning is a threat. Symptoms of poisoning may include drowsiness; changes in behavior, like shivering or staggering; bleeding at the mouth or another body opening; and breathing problems, such as panting and gasping. Time is of the essence here: poisoning requires immediate treatment. If you know what the dog has ingested, you may be able to help him yourself.

For dogs who have raided the medicine cabinet, chewed up crayons from the toy chest, or got under the sink to eat kitchen matches or insecticides, you should try to induce vomiting.

The best way to get a dog to vomit is to administer hydrogen peroxide, one teaspoonful for each ten pounds of body weight. The dog should start vomiting within five minutes. You can try again ten minutes later, if you don't have success the first time. But, at this point, you should also be on your way to the veterinarian's office. Only try to induce vomiting if you are absolutely sure what your dog has ingested. You never want a dog to bring up drain cleaner or kerosene. These caustic substances can burn his throat and esophagus when he vomits. If you have any doubts at all about what the dog may have swallowed, get him to the veterinarian right away.

SOMETHING IN THE EAR

Frolicking in the great outdoors is wonderful for your dog but you should always conduct a body scan when you return from your walks. In many parts of the country, disease-bearing ticks are a serious problem (See Lyme Disease on page 00). But even seeds, pebbles, and other small objects can get caught in the ear and cause your dog difficulties. Sometimes you can see the object easily, and using blunt-edged tweezers, you can remove it quickly. At other times, the problem is trickier. A dog who keeps shaking her head and trying to scratch at her ear after a walk outdoors is giving you clues.

Only a veterinarian can safely removed an object that is deeply lodged, but you can soothe the dog's discomfort by pouring olive oil or mineral oil into the ear. Sometimes the oil will loosen the object and float it up into the outer ear where it can be easily removed. But don't wait too long. If you don't have luck quickly, call the veterinarian.

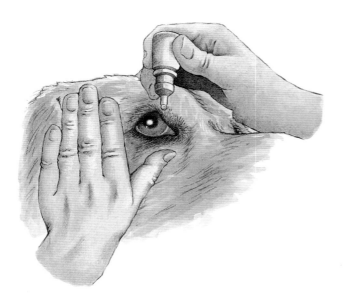

SOMETHING IN THE EYE

Windy days are especially hazardous, but most dogs who play actively and roll on the ground can get something caught in their eye without much difficulty, even in the calmest of weather.

To float out the debris, try holding the dog's eye wide open and use eye drops, either sterile contact lens solution or an eye rinse for dry eyes, to get things moving. If that doesn't work, or if there are any signs that the dog's eyeball is scratched or cut, take him to the veterinarian right away.

When You Must See the Vet

Gastrointestinal problems	Poisoning (can cause death within hours unless it is treated)
	When vomiting and/or diarrhea last for more than a day, they can cause dehydration: rehydration is critical.
	Whenever you see blood in vomit or in the dog's stool, call the veterinarian.
	Bloating, major changes in water consumption, watery stools or tar-like stools
Bleeding	Bleeding at the area of the wrist behind the paw (could signal a severed artery)
	Spurting blood: Any bleeding that doesn't stop when pressure is applied requires immediate veterinary attention
Choking	When your best first aid efforts—including the Heimlich Maneuver and CPR—don't work, get to the vet right away
Traumatic injury	Anything, including car accidents, dog fights, and puncture wounds, should be examined by your vet
Shock or seizure	If your dog fails to respond to your voice or will not wake up, go to the veterinarian
Fever	If your dog's temperature stays at 103 degrees or higher for more than two days, or if her temperature drops below 100 degrees, call the veterinarian.

SNAKE BITES AND INSECT STINGS

You probably won't see a snake bite on your dog. You are more likely to notice the after-effects. A dog who is drooling, shaking, vomiting, or who's acting agitated and shows dilated pupils may be the victim of a poisonous snakebite. Try to find the place on the dog's body where he has been bitten. Apply an ice pack to the wound to reduce swelling and to slow down the flow of blood. Do not try to cut into the wound or suck out the venom. Call your veterinarian immediately.

Dogs love to chase anything that moves, and bees, wasps, and hornets fight back. Bees usually leave a stinger embedded in the dog's skin. Using a magnifying glass and a blunt-edged tweezers, pull the stinger out. Then, apply an ice pack to reduce the swelling. Wasp and hornet stings can be more serious because some dogs are allergic to them. Get the dog to the veterinarian immediately if you notice any swelling around the mouth or the throat. If you're not sure what kind of insect has stung your dog, call the veterinarian.

CARDIOPULMONARY RESUSCITATION (CPR AND RESCUE BREATHING)

CPR is the method used to treat an animal who is not breathing, who has lost consciousness, or who has no heartbeat. It consists of rescue breathing (also called mouth-to-mouth resuscitation) and chest compressions. CPR is based on three principles, called the ABCs of CPR. You must follow the ABC order (Airway, Breathing, and Circulation) when attempting CPR.

A IS FOR AIRWAY

Is the dog's airway open? The airway is the passage through which the animal breathes. Check to see if the throat and mouth are clear of foreign objects. If the answer is YES, go to Breathing. If the answer is NO, you need to open the airway. Be very careful about placing your fingers inside the mouth of a conscious animal—you could be bitten. Try to calm the animal before attempting the following:

1. Lay the dog down, on either side.
2. Gently tilt the head slightly back to extend the neck and head.
3. Pull the tongue between the front teeth.
4. Use your finger to check for and remove any foreign object or vomit from the mouth.

Packing a First-Class First-Aid Kit

A first-aid kit should always be readily accessible, and include the following items:

❧ Equipment   Gauze bandages and dressing pads (many sizes) to clean wounds, apply pressure, and make bandages

Adhesive tape to secure bandages

Cotton swabs to clean wounds or apply ointments

Tweezers to remove foreign objects like thorns or splinters

Paper towels

Pediatric rectal thermometer to take the dog's temperature

Material for making a splint (i.e., a piece of wood, newspaper, sticks, popsicle sticks, or tongue depressors, etc.)

Grooming clippers or blunt-end scissors to cut hair away from wounds

Towel

Thermal or regular blanket

Strong packing tape (for taping a broken leg to a firm surface)

Roll bandages or gauze to wrap wounds or make a muzzle

Flashlight

Eyedropper

❧ Medicine   3 percent hydrogen peroxide (can be given orally at one teaspoon per ten pounds to induce vomiting)

Antibacterial ointment

Sterile eyewash or lubricant

Milk of magnesia

K-Y jelly

❧ Reference Material   *Pet First Aid: Cats and Dogs* by Bobbie Mammato, DVM, MPH, produced by The Humane Society and the American Red Cross.

Vital Information Card with any allergies or special health conditions your dog has and with phone numbers for your veterinarian, for the nearest emergency pet clinic, and the National Animal Poison Control Center.

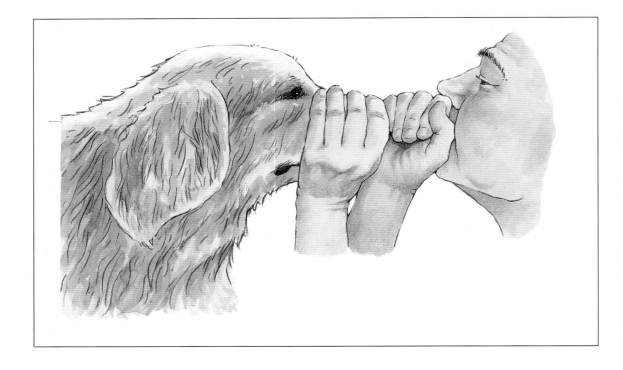

B IS FOR BREATHING

Is the dog breathing? If the answer is YES, allow the dog to get into a comfortable body position. Then move onto Circulation. If the answer is NO, do the following:

1. Check that the airway is open. (See Airway, above)

2. Make sure the dog's neck is stretched forward. Then, cup your hands and mouth over the dog's nose and forcefully exhale.

3. Breathe into the nostrils for about three seconds to inflate the lungs. Pause for two seconds. Repeat. Do this four or five times, then check to see if your pet is breathing.

4. If the dog begins to breathe, but the breathing is shallow and irregular, or if breathing does not begin, continue to practice artificial respiration until you reach the veterinarian or veterinary hospital.

C IS FOR CIRCULATION

Is there a heartbeat or a pulse? To check, lie the dog down on the right side. Feel behind the dog's elbow with your hand or place your ear on the dog's chest. If the answer is YES, continue to perform mouth-to-mouth resuscitation. If the answer is NO, perform chest compressions, also called cardiac massage. Do not assume there is no heartbeat or pulse simply because the dog is not breathing. Do not start chest compressions before checking for a heartbeat. (If the animal is conscious and responds to you, the heart is beating.) Here's how to perform cardiac massage on your dog:

1. Lay the dog down on the right side.
2. Kneel next to your dog with the animal's chest facing you.
3. Place the palm of one of your hands over the ribs at the point where the elbow touches the chest. Place your other hand on top and firmly press both hands down and forward toward the brain. This squeezes blood out of the heart to the brain.
4. Repeat six times at one-second intervals. Then, stop and return to assisted breathing technique.
5. If you are working alone, do six compressions for each breath, then check for a pulse by placing two fingers as high as possible on the inside of either leg, just where the leg meets the body. (A light touch best allows you to pick up the pulse.)
6. If there are two people, one person should perform the breathing technique while the other performs the chest compressions at a rate of two or three compressions for each breath, then check for a pulse.

Continue CPR until the dog has a strong heart beat and pulse, or until you reach the veterinary hospital.

NATURAL REMEDIES

Starting with good nutrition as a basis for holistic health, natural medicine stresses a shared responsibility—between lay persons and health care professionals—for an animal's overall well-being.

CHAPTER SIX

five holistic healing therapies

Homeopathy. Ayurveda. Chinese medicine. You've probably heard of these forms of natural healing. In fact, you may well be among the millions of Americans today who use natural remedies for their own health care. Drug store shelves are full of natural health care products and major pharmaceutical companies now produce lines of herbal medicines. The growing interest in natural health care has implications for animals as well as humans. As more pet owners are using natural medicine in their own health care, they are looking for holistic healing techniques to treat their animal companions. Many veterinarians are learning about acupuncture, herbal medicine, and other natural therapies and opening practices that specialize in these healing techniques.

What's the attraction of natural medicine? It's an alternative system of healthcare with gentle, effective methods. These remedies don't have the adverse side effects that powerful drugs often do. Starting with good nutrition as a basis for holistic health, natural medicine stresses a shared responsibility—between lay persons and health care professionals—for an animal's overall well-being.

More and more people are using alternative therapies to help them stay well and to treat chronic health problems. People are also finding new and successful approaches to maintaining and improving their dogs' health and well-being. A natural approach to canine care begins with a consideration of the dog's health history, personality, age, sex, and breed characteristics. The dog's environment, including his diet, exercise routine, and housing are also taken into consideration before any prescription is made. Holistic veterinarians pay particular attention to the relationships the dog has with the people and other animals who share his home. All of these factors are part of the equation. Whether the holistic veterinarian decides to use acupuncture, herbal remedies, or Bach flower remedies depends on a balanced assessment of the many aspects of a dog's life. The following are alternative therapies holistic veterinarians most commonly prescribe.

ACUPUNCTURE

Acupuncture is not a revolutionary new breakthrough in medicine. Chinese practitioners have used this treatment—on both humans and animals—for thousands of years. Ancient practitioners theorized that an energy force, called *qi* (*chi*), flows through bodies along twelve special channels called meridians. As long as the energy force flows freely, the body remains healthy. But when these meridians get blocked, the body becomes ill. To get the force flowing, acupuncturists insert fine needles into specific areas of the body. Practitioners say that acupuncture works through the central nervous system and affects the musculoskeletal, hormonal, and cardiovascular systems.

Studies repeatedly show that acupuncture aids circulation and triggers the release of many neurotransmitters and neurohormones—some of which are endorphins, the body's natural pain killers. As a result, acupuncture can relieve muscle spasms and stimulate the nerves and the body's defense system.

For dogs, the acupuncturist inserts the tiny, sterile needles into the appropriate points of the animal's body as quickly and calmly as possible so as not to disturb the dog. The most common points stimulated are on the front paws and the hind legs. There are also points around the head and the back. A treatment can be as brief as ten seconds or last as long as thirty minutes, depending on the condition that's being treated. The therapy schedule may call for appointments one to three times per week for a period of four to six weeks.

Many holistic veterinarians use acupuncture as part of a "geriatric tune-up." It seems to help older dogs who aren't eating well or who are acting lethargic. Acupuncture is often helpful in the treatment of chronic kidney disease, liver disease, arthritis, and respiratory problems when mainstream therapies aren't working. Because acupuncture stimulates the body's own system of healing and because no chemicals are administered, there are no side effects and complications rarely develop. (The International Veterinary Acupuncture Society (IVAS) certifies veterinary acupuncturists. For more information, contact IVAS at 268 West 3rd Street, Nederland, CO 80466.)

HERBAL MEDICINES

Herbalists who treat canines generally assume that you are already feeding your dog a nutritious diet. Proper nutrition and herbal healing go hand in hand. Herbs are, after all, plants that can also be used to season and garnish food. As healing agents, herbs have been used for thousands of years in civilizations as diverse as the Egyptians, Greeks, Romans, Arabs, and Chinese. In modern times, scientists have turned to herbal ingredients to create many of our most common pharmaceutical drugs. Digitalis, for instance, is a derivative of foxglove, while cortisone comes from the yucca plant. Today, scientists continue to explore the benefits of phyto-medicines, the healing power of plants.

Herbs are frequently used by veterinarians who prefer natural products to chemical substances. Pennyroyal and mint-filled collars, for instance, can be used in flea season to substitute for toxic chemicals. Herbs can be used to treat dogs with skin problems, kidney and bladder trouble, arthritis, anemia, diabetes, wounds and fractures, constipation, diarrhea, and even heart and lung problems. They can also be used as antispasmodics and mild tranquilizers.

It's best to use freshly gathered herbs if you are going to prepare your own remedies. But herbal preparations sold in pet stores and natural food stores can also be helpful. It is best to introduce herbal medicines under a veterinarian's supervision since some herbs can be poisonous to dogs and others may interact with food or prescription medications your dog is taking.

AYURVEDA

Ayurveda is the oldest medical system in the world. Its healing principles, discovered in India 5,000 years ago, have influenced the development of all subsequent medical traditions, including traditional Chinese medicine and

Various Herbs Used by Holistic Veterinarians

HERB	WHAT IT'S USED FOR
Aloe	Minor burns, skin irritations, stomach disorders
Borage	Fever, inflammation, respiratory infections, stress
Bupleurum	Fever, irritability
Chamomile	Anxiety, flatulence, indigestion, inflammation, healing of wounds
Comfrey	Bruises, burns, ulcers, healing wounds (for external use only)
Echinacea	Viral and bacterial illnesses, eczema, skin problems
Fennel	Colic, flatulence, indigestion, coughs
Garlic	Common cold, coughs, adenoid problems, respiratory infections, bacterial infections
Ginger	Motion sickness, dizziness, digestion
Goldenseal	Digestion, inflammation, infection
Hawthorn	Insomnia, heart trouble, nervousness
Lavender	Nervous exhaustion, insomnia, rheumatic pain
Marigold	Bruise, burns, healing wounds, skin inflammation, conjunctivitis, some fungal infections, adenoid problems
Milk Thistle	Liver disorders, psoriasis
Mullen	Diarrhea, hemorrhoids, bronchitis, coughs
Nettle	Constipation, allergies
Peppermint	Indigestion, nausea
Red Raspberry	Diarrhea, nausea, vomiting
Rosemary	Headache, muscular pain, neuralgia, general debility, digestive problems
Tangerine Peel	Digestion
White Willow	Fever and inflammation
Yarrow	Wounds, high blood pressure

Is Your Dog Vata, Pitta, or Kapha?

To understand Ayurveda, it's important to know something about the *doshas*, the constitutional types that are the building blocks for therapeutic treatment in this medical system. Dosha has something in common with the Western notion of body types: ectomorph (light and slim), endomorph (heavy and soft), and mesomorph (husky and muscular). But the Ayurvedic typology adds to these physical descriptions layers of information about emotional tendencies, intelligence, and spiritual inclinations.

There are three doshas: *vata, pitta*, and *kapha*. Although everything in nature is a mix of all three, one dosha usually predominates. The following descriptions should help you determine your dog's dosha.

❧ Skittish *Vata*

The vata dog is light, cool, clear, and closely connected to the element of air. Vata dogs are usually thin with a prominent bone structure and may be prone to dry skin. High-strung by nature, they can be nervous and fearful of loud noises and strangers. The greyhound is a good example of a vata dog.

❧ High-Energy *Pitta*

The pitta dog is a fiery creature, strong-willed and alert. Physically, pitta is muscular and usually has a short-haired, wiry coat. The Airedale terrier is a good example of a pitta dog.

❧ Sweet, Soulful *Kapha*

Sensuous, calm, sweet-natured and easygoing, kapha tends to have a well-developed body with large, but not prominent, bones. The coat is lush, long-haired, and often wavy or curly. A golden retriever is a good example of a kapha dog.

Western medicine. A spiritual system as well as a medical one, Ayurveda traces its beginnings to the wisdom of the sages, called *rishis*, who received the principles while in deep states of meditation.

Ayurveda assumes that everything in the universe is filled with consciousness and is evolving toward enlightenment. That includes your dog! Ayurvedic philosophers ask you to picture the universe as an immense ocean upon which individual beings rise and fall like waves. Even rocks and clouds have consciousness in Ayurvedic terms. As a higher form of life, animals are imbued with more of the cosmic energy all beings share. Human beings might vibrate at a quicker mental frequency than dogs do, but our animal companions may be more spiritually evolved than we are. As holistic vets point out, animals are in better balance with nature.

Like other holistic healing systems, Ayurveda recommends a fresh, whole-foods diet. Humans who follow Ayurvedic principles are frequently vegetarian, but cutting meat out of your dog's diet isn't necessary, or even recommended. Ayurveda stresses that all creatures should live by principles that are natural to them.

Eating foods that will balance the *dosha*, or the constitutional type each dog personifies (see Is Your Dog *Vata, Pitta,* or *Kapha* on page 72) is the goal. One dog's digestion might be improved by adding a little ginger to her food, while another will benefit from drinking plenty of water, and a third may need to eat more heavy, oily food.

Because Ayurveda is a holistic approach to health and wellness, its prescriptions include meditation practices, exercises like yoga, suggestions for daily routines—including when to awaken and what kind of music to listen to—as well as dietary and medicinal remèdies. Dogs can skip the meditation, Ayurvedic vets say, and they instinctively practice their own form of yoga.

Ayurveda also focuses on relationships between beings. While your dog won't sit down to meditate, you might consider making a meditation session part of your daily routine. The calmer state of mind that you develop as a result of regular meditation will improve your relationship with your dog. Treating your dog with love and kindness goes a long way toward keeping her well. And taking good care of yourself is another fine way to care for your canine companion. Dogs are so sensitive to their guardian's mood and frame of mind that your own peace and happiness has a major impact on them.

The underlying principle of Ayurvedic medicine is balance. Getting the body into balance is the goal, accomplished with detoxification (called *panchakarma*), diet, and slow, gentle healing techniques that emphasize prevention. Veterinarians who use Ayurveda tend to specialize in their practices. They use Ayurvedic herbs to help cleanse the system as part of a panchakarma process that may also include some fasting and oil massages. (Left to her own devices, your dog would probably not initiate a fast. Although a short, twenty-four-hour, fast is unlikely to do any harm, the decision to put a dog on one should be made in conjunction with your veterinarian.) Dietary prescriptions often help lethargic older dogs regain youthful energy. Massages are also healing and a wonderful way for humans and dogs to bond.

BACH FLOWER REMEDIES

We send flowers to friends in the hospital and buy ourselves bouquets when we're feeling down. Our canine companions love to frolic in fields of flowers, rolling around and luxuriating in the sensations and the scents. Dr. Edward Bach, an English physician, took this "flower power" further in the 1920s and 1930s when he began observing the healing effects of certain flower essences on his human patients. Dr. Bach noticed that many of his patients exhibited emotional difficulties such as apprehension, worry, loneliness, or anxiety before becoming physically ill. So, he became convinced that if these emotions were alleviated, the patient's body would have more strength for healing itself.

Bach determined that the best remedies for these emotional and mental problems were found in the flowers that grew in the fields and on the trees of his native English countryside. He succeeded in identifying thirty-eight plant remedies that he divided into seven groups, according to the problems they treat. These flower essences, preserved in brandy, can be found at natural food stores and at herbalists. Holistic veterinarians say that animals respond more readily to the flower essences because they are closer to nature and more open to the subtle healing process.

Flower essences are different from other kinds of medicine because they aren't intended to treat physical illnesses directly. Instead, they are used for healing emotional problems. According to holistic vets, yarrow is one of the more effective flower essences for use with animals. Rescue Remedy, also called Five-Flower Remedy and Emergency Formula, is made from cherry plum, clematis, rock rose, impatiens, and star-of-Bethlehem. It can be used in stressful situations, such as a trip to the veterinarian, or to help an overexcited dog calm down. Chamomile is good for digestive problems, and borage helps lift depression.

Holistic veterinarians can prescribe the right flower essence for your dog in a particular situation. You can also study the use of the flower remedies (there are many books on the subject) and learn to trust your own instincts about their use. To avoid having your dog lick the essences, which could upset her stomach, veterinarians recommend that you apply a few drops to the top of her head where she can't reach it. The subtle effects of the flower essences build over time, so it's often a good idea to repeat treatments every few hours for two or three days.

TRADITIONAL CHINESE MEDICINE (TCM)

Traditional Chinese Medicine (TCM) is a complex tradition of treatment that has evolved over thousands of years. It is a dynamic system that takes into account both internal and external aspects of health. The body, mind, and spirit as well as heredity factors, stress, and even the climate and the time of year factor into a patient's treatment plan. When most people think of Chinese medicine, they think of acupuncture. This most familiar aspect of TCM is widely used with great success to treat dogs that suffer form arthritis pain, constipation, loss of appetite, and chronic disease.

TCM combines acupuncture, herbs, diet, meditation, and exercise for a holistic approach to healing. With the exception of meditation and exercise, all these therapies work as well for animals as they do for humans. In China, farm animals have been treated with acupuncture, herbs, and food medicine for generations. Since the 1970s, when China opened its doors to trade with the West, TCM has developed a loyal U.S. following among veterinarians as well as physicians.

Chinese herbal medicine is not as well known as acupuncture but it is an integral part of TCM. Chinese herbalists use diagnostic methods that are very different from Western techniques. They observe the tongue, the pulse, the eyes, the hair, and the skin and draw conclusions from what they see, hear, and feel. Chinese medical treatment is highly individualized. What causes one dog to sneeze, for example, could be completely different from what causes the identical symptom in another dog. The treatments recommended will therefore be entirely different.

Prevention is the key in Chinese medicine. The TCM philosophy maintains that disease is caused by imbalances of the vital force or energy, also known as qi (chi). Imbalances often swing toward one end of a spectrum between hot and cold or wet and dry—similar to the Chinese concepts of yin and yang. If imbalances are detected and treated early, the problem can be resolved before a serious disease develops.

To help practitioners detect imbalances, TCM assigns an intricate set of affiliations between natural elements and parts of the body, incorporating variations in time of day, season, emotions, colors, foods, odor, and directions. Everything is connected! The Chinese herbalist takes all these relationships into consideration when prescribing a remedy.

Because the system is so complex, there are very few herbal treatments that a lay person can safely use. There can be fifteen or more herbs in one formula medicine and each plays a different role. All have powerful pharmacological effects and so they should not be used without professional supervision. Ma Huang, for instance, is a strong stimulant used to treat respiratory disease. Some dogs can tolerate the stimulating effects, but others become frantic.

To find a veterinarian who is qualified to practice TCM, contact the International Veterinary Acupuncture Society (IVAS). IVAS has certified hundreds of veterinary acupuncturists in the United States and the organization also offers a three-year course on Chinese herbs to veterinarians who have already been trained in acupuncture. (See page 135 for more information on contacting IVAS.)

Homeopathic First-Aid Kit

Here are a few homeopathic items you'll want to keep on hand for your dog. See the chart on page 77 for an expanded list of homeopathic remedies and what they are used for.

- Aconite for emotional stress
- Apis for bites and stings
- Arnica for bruises and swelling
- Carbo Veg for flatulence and digestive disorders
- Hypericum for cuts and scratches

Various Homeopathic Remedies for Dogs and What They're Used For

REMEDY	WHAT IT'S USED FOR
Aconite	Angina, arrhythmia, arthritis, asthma, colds, fevers, eye inflammations, middle ear infections, toothache
Allium cepa	Colds with sinus congestion, coughs, watery and inflamed eyes, earaches
Apis	Insect stings, cystitis, edema, arthritis, allergic reactions in eyes, throat, mouth (Avoid if your dog is pregnant)
Argentum nit.	To combat fear before a big event such as a kennel show
Arnica	Broken bones, sprains, strains, and other sudden injuries with swelling, tenderness, sore and swollen joints, toothache
Arsenicum alb.	Fear and panic, food poisoning with severe vomiting or diarrhea
Belladonna	Feverish colds, sore throat, earache, high fever and abscesses
Bryonia	Swollen painful joints, heat exhaustion, nausea, colds
Calcarea Carbonica	Broken bones, sprains, muscle cramps, constipation, chronic ear infections, eye inflammations, headaches, insomnia, allergies, gastritis, menstrual problems, asthma, arthritis
Cantharis	Burns, scalds, any burning or stinging sensation
Chamomilla	Extreme pain or irritability, pain following surgery or dental work, insomnia, restlessness
Ferrum phosphoricum	Tickling, hacking cough with chest pain, headaches, fevers, ear infections, rheumatic joints, anemia, fatigue, nosebleeds, sore throat, vomiting, diarrhea, palpitations
Gelsemium	Fear, influenza, sneezing, absence of thirst but a need to urinate often
Hypericum	Wounds with shooting pain, injuries where nerves are affected, head wounds, nausea, indigestion, diarrhea
Ipecac	Nausea, vomiting, asthma, cough accompanied by wheezing, diarrhea, flu with nausea, gastroenteritis
Kali bichromicum	Acute, bronchitis, sinusitis, and resulting headaches, indigestion, pains in the joints
Lachesis	Choking coughs, croup, earaches, indigestion, insomnia, hot flashes, heart arrhythmia
Ledum	Insect stings, puncture wounds, including immunization and surgery, prevents infection
Lycopodium	Colds, constipation, coughs, indigestion, gas, heartburn, joint pain, sciatica
Mercurius vivus	Abscesses, colds with an exceptionally runny nose, painful diarrhea, influenza, earache with discharge of pus, eye inflammation, indigestion, mouth ulcers
Rhus	Red, swollen, itchy blisters, painful stiff muscles, cramp, rheumatic or arthritis pain
Ruta grav.	Pain and stiffness, eye strain, rheumatism, sciatica
Silicia	Splinters that could cause infection, recurrent colds and infections, weak nails, fractures

CHAPTER SEVEN

holistic healing and preventive care

To make the most of your dog's later years, preventive health care is essential. Alternative healing systems such as TCM and Ayurveda focus on preventive care. But you don't have to adopt an entire system of healing to provide the preventive medicine your dog needs. Bodywork, especially chiropractic, Tellington T Touch (pronounced Tee-Touch), and Reiki massage can help you and your veterinarian monitor your dog's condition and simultaneously enhance his well-being.

Learning animal communication techniques can bring you into closer harmony with your dog's mind and spirit. And aromatherapy provides soothing remedies and tonics to keep your dog feeling happy and relaxed.

CHIROPRACTIC

Chiropractic is based on the theory that the proper function of the spinal cord and the nervous system housed within it are the keys to good health. Chiropractors believe that adequate nerve supply from the spinal column is essential to maintain good health.

Picture the nervous system as the communication line within the body. It carries information back and forth between the brain and the cells. The main line housing this system is the spinal column, which is made up of bones called vertebrae. Each vertebra encases part of the nervous system. The spinal cord passes through the center of each bone. Nerves branch off the spinal cord and exit between two vertebrae to travel to all the muscles and organs in the body.

But if the vertebral bones in the spine are misaligned—even very slightly—they can affect the functioning of the nerves and inhibit the flow of energy, throwing off normal biomechanical and neurological performance throughout the body. When a misaligned vertebra gets stuck, it's called a subluxation. Subluxations pinch off or alter the flow of information from the brain. It's the chiropractor's job to "adjust" them by manipulating the stuck vertebra back into position to restore proper alignment of the spine.

Chiropractic has become the most popular alternative medical therapy in the United States. But humans aren't the only creatures whose bodies need adjustments from time to time. Any animal with a spine, from a peppy Chihuahua to a regal racehorse, can benefit from chiropractic, a drugless method of healing that utilizes the recuperative powers of the body to heal itself. Spinal adjustments have been done on horses for more than one hundred years, but the practice has only recently

become popular with dog owners. Dogs, like horses, are susceptible to back and disc problems. Keeping dogs on leashes—like horses on bridles—adds to the potential for problems.

Dogs have a natural tendency to stretch and work out the kinks they may develop from being on a leash, but chiropractic care can help them when that natural self-healing practice isn't enough. Back pain is the most obvious condition that chiropractic treatment helps. A dog who is stiff or limping may be suffering from back pain; a dog who shies away from petting may be doing so because his back hurts. But don't wait until back pain is evident—any change in gait or flexibility is a signal that your dog could benefit from a chiropractic check-up.

Regular chiropractic sessions can help keep a dog limber. Also, many different problems or situations can cause a dog's vertebrae to go out of whack and make that dog a candidate for chiropractic treatment. Among the problems that chiropractic can effectively treat are:

• Trauma from a fall, misstep, accident, fight, or even just a spill on the ice

• Stiffness and reduced mobility due to old age

• Arthritis

• Epilepsy

• Gastrointestinal blockage

While chiropractic adjustment may be just what the doctor ordered for your dog, before starting any such treatment, make sure a doctor does indeed order it. A general veterinary examination and evaluation is recommended before beginning any chiropractic treatment. You want to make sure to rule out any medical problems requiring acute care before you begin treatments—you don't want to be treating a dog with chiropractic adjust-ments when the real problem is a compound fracture or an ear infection. A pre-chiropractic veterinary work-up might include blood work, urinalysis, x-rays, or a bone or CAT scan, depending on your dog's symptoms.

Once a veterinarian has examined your dog, he or she might suggest chiropractic care as an alternative or adjunct to traditional treatment plans. Then, it is crucial to find a qualified practitioner who knows and understands both chiropractic and veterinary medicine. The practitioner should be a veterinarian with a certificate in chiropractic animal care, or should be a licensed Doctor of Chiropractic (DC) working under the auspices of a veterinarian. (For more information on veterinary chiropractic and to find out about practitioners in your area, contact the American Veterinary Chiropractic Association (AVCA), a national organization that certifies practitioners and offers educational programs in animal chiropractic. Write to the AVCA at 623 Main Street, Hillsdale, Illinois 61257.)

TELLINGTON TTOUCH

No one knows exactly how Tellington TTouch (Tee-Touch) works, not even Linda Tellington-Jones, the horse trainer and animal therapist who invented it in the mid 1970s. Tellington Ttouch borrows some ideas from Chinese medicine, but for the most part, this technique is Tellington-Jones' own invention. Tellington TTouch has been used to treat behavioral problems, to speed recovery from illness or injury, and to help animal athletes achieve peak performance. Tellington-Jones has worked with zookeepers, Olympic equestrian trainers, and veterinarians. She has also produced books and videos on her method.

TTouch is a series of massaging movements, mostly applied in clockwise circles, using a variety of hand positions and pressures. Different movements are designed to

relieve specific problems. The strokes are all named after animals. "Lick of the Cow's Tongue," for instance, is recommended to stop excessive barking. The most basic TTouch move, "The Clouded Leopard," is used to relieve pain and swelling. Holding your hands in a relaxed cupped or curved position, you move the pads of your fingers in small, clockwise one and one-quarter circles around the affected part of the animal's body. Pressure and speed vary, depending on the condition being treated and the size of the animal.

Critics say that Tellington TTouch works because owners touch their animals more frequently when they are practicing this technique, that the comfort of any kind of touch has a healing effect. But Tellington-Jones' research shows difference in brain-wave patterns during TTouch and traditional massage, petting, and stroking. She claims that her technique works because it stimulates neurons and wakes up brain waves, enhancing health and well-being. She also likes the way that TTouch opens up channels of communication between humans and animals and believes that there are benefits to be gained in this interaction for humans as well as the animals. (For more information on Tellington TTouch, call 1-800-797-PETS.)

REIKI

The term Reiki is a combination of two Japanese words, *rei* and *ki*, which together mean universal energy. Created by a nineteenth-century Japanese minister, practitioners say that Reiki awakens and enlivens the spiritual consciousness that animates all living things. There are some Reiki masters who treat animals as well as humans.

Reiki can be used alone or in conjunction with another holistic modality such as massage or chiropractic.

Practitioners may begin by focusing attention on an area where the dog has been injured or where an illness is centered. Then they will allow their instincts to guide them to other parts of the body where the Reiki energy is needed.

Reiki practitioners enter a meditative state and allow the "universal energy" to pass through the channels of their hands. Unlike massage or chiropractic, Reiki does not involve pressure, palpation, or kneading. Only the lightest touch is necessary to impart healing energy. In some cases, practitioners just allow their hands to hover over the body. In fact, Reiki practitioners do not even have to be in the same room with a patient to have healing take place. Reiki can be done from afar; distance is not a factor.

Reiki is most frequently used to treat animals who have suffered accidents or injuries. Practitioners claim that the technique is particularly helpful for bringing injured animals out of shock. But Reiki can also be used to help treat life-threatening diseases such as cancer. While it is not a primary treatment in these cases, it can help relieve pain and release vital energy so that the animal's immune system is strengthened, according to practitioners.

Reiki practitioners never push their services on anyone. Whether the patient is a human or an animal, the trained Reiki practitioner waits for the patient to ask for help. A dog may come and sit near the practitioner's hands, for instance, signifying that she wishes to be treated. (There is no definitive source of information on Reiki treatment for dogs but a good place to start is at http://www.holistichound.com. Free long-distance Reiki healings for pets are available via the web at www.nucleus.com/~gateway/pets.)

Massage for Dogs

Everyone knows that dogs love to be touched. Petting and stroking a dog is a crucial part of the human-animal relationship. But most petting centers around the head and shoulder regions. Some people take a rough approach to petting, literally slapping the dog on the back or ruffling its fur. Massage approaches touching in a gentler, more mindful way. Dogs love the extended contact and people who massage their dogs find that it relaxes both the dog and them.

Begin by thinking about what parts of her body your dog most likes to have touched. Find a comfortable place on a carpeted floor. With your dog in a seated position, begin at the head, gently massaging the eyelids, muzzle, and nose. From there, work down the neck to the chest and pectoral muscles. Use long, firm strokes. Your dog may offer her paw. You can accept it, but gently put it down again if your dog loses her balance.

The dog may lie down so that her belly can be stroked. Don't forget to massage your dog's legs, too.

Massage can help dogs who are recovering from injuries or fractures get well more quickly. It can also help to restore muscle tone and help calm a stressed dog. Use your intuition and follow your dog's communications about what she likes and dislikes. Try to keep the stroking firm and methodical so that your dog comes to know the difference between getting a massage and just being petted.

HOMEOPATHY

Homeopathy is a system of holistic medicine that uses small doses of natural substances to stimulate the body's natural defense system. It was developed in the early 1800s by the German physician Samuel Hahnemann. Hahnemann's premise was that "like cures like" and he determined that a remedy should produce in a healthy person the same symptoms as the illness it is intended to cure. If, for example, a patient has red, irritated eyes and a runny nose, the treatment might consist of diluted onion juice, which produces the same symptoms when administered in large doses. In an infintesimal dose, however, homeopaths claim that the substance has a paradoxical effect: that is, it cures what it might, in larger dose, cause.

Hahnemann's research showed that homeopathic remedies are more effective when they are highly diluted with alcohol or water and repeatedly agitated. At times, a substance may be so diluted that only a minuscule amount enters the patient's body. But, to homeopaths, the medicine still contains the healing essence of the original substance.

Homeopaths believe that if they can match the pattern of the remedy close enough to the pattern of the disease, an internal mechanism stimulates the body to heal itself. Homeopaths choose from more than one thousand remedies, hundreds of which are used on a regular basis. Some of the most common homeopathic remedies used to treat dogs are:

- Arsenicum album (white oxide of arsenic)
- Nux vomica (arsenic)
- Arnica (leopard's bone)
- Stramonium (thorn apple)
- Pulsatilla (windflower)
- Rhus toxicodendron (poison ivy)

At first glance, these remedies might sound more dangerous than the diseases they are meant to cure. But it's important to remember how repeatedly the substances are diluted before being used. At times, the substance has been diluted and agitated so many times that it seems physically impossible for the original substance to be part of the mix. But, homeopaths believe that the remedy may even gain strength as the substance is diluted.

To decide how to treat a dog, the homeopath looks for all of the signals that a disease displays, whether the symptoms are mental, emotional, or physical. The goal of the homeopath is to treat the whole dog and not just the individual symptoms. In a preliminary session with the owner, the homeopath asks for a detailed description of what is wrong with the dog. The practitioner will also want to know other things about the dog. Is he afraid of lightning? How much water does he drink? At what time of day is he happiest? Does she chew her right paw when she's upset? All of these little details that a conventional practitioner may have no interest in can become keys to treatment for the homeopath in search of the right remedy.

Once homeopaths have identified all the symptoms, they then look for the homeopathic picture that includes those symptoms. The dog may have a fear of loud noises or might startle easily. There may be twenty different remedies for that symptom. Then the dog's need for a lot of water is plugged in; that may narrow the list to fifteen remedies. As each symptom is added, the list narrows until finally there is a match. Homeopaths give one remedy at a time, depending on the "picture" the animal presents, and they use special reference books, such as the *Materia Medica*, which catalogues the effects of countless substances.

Depending on many factors, particularly the severity of the disease and the length of time the dog has been suffering, treatment time will vary. For chronic diseases, treatment can last for a year or more. With older dogs, treatments may take longer than with younger dogs because their systems take longer to heal. You can buy homeopathic remedies for your dog at some pet stores and natural food stores, but generally these remedies are only good for temporary relief. For overall cures, it's best to consult with a qualified homeopathic veterinarian who can set up a treatment plan. (For a list of homeopathic veterinarians trained by Richard H. Pitcairn, DVM, Ph.D., president of the Academy of Veterinary Homeopathy, send a self-addressed, stamped envelope to the Academy of Veterinary Homeopathy, 1283 Lincoln St., Eugene, OR 97401.)

AROMATHERAPY

Aromatherapy uses the aromatic essences of plants to achieve a specific physical, emotional, mental, or spiritual effect. Like other holistic therapies, aromatherapy has been practiced since the earliest days of civilization. The Egyptians used essential oils both for the well-being of the living and to soothe the spirits of the dead. The ancient Greeks, with their emphasis on beauty and physical well-being, were lavish in their use of aromatic oils.

Essential oils are derived from different parts of plants such as the leaves, the flowers, the roots, and the bark. Certain plants can produce a number of oils, depending on the parts that are used. With citrus trees, for example, orange oil is extracted from the peel of the fruit, petitgrain comes from the leaves or twigs, and neroli is produced from the blossoms. Aromatherapists use the oils in a variety of ways. The scents can be inhaled for healing purposes or a few drops of oil can be added to bath water. Dilutions of essential oils can also be applied directly to the skin.

> ### Seven Steps to Communicating with Your Dog
>
> ❧ Observe your dog quietly, letting your mind become calm and open to perceive and receive messages clearly.
>
> ❧ Visualize something, and send it to your dog's body.
>
> ❧ Get your dog's attention, and send a hello or other message or image.
>
> ❧ Say hello, and imagine your dog saying hello back to you.
>
> ❧ Ask a question, and accept whatever communications you receive from your dog.
>
> ❧ Acknowledge the answer.
>
> ❧ Practice with other questions at other times.

Research on aromatherapy tends to be limited to its use with humans, but holistic veterinarians believe that the healing effects also apply to animals. There are oils, for example, that seem to be sedating and oils that are antiseptic. The same oils may not work in exactly the same ways on dogs as they do on humans, however. Lavender, for instance, has calming effects for many people but doesn't seem to soothe dogs as much. Holistic veterinarians believe that there's a mind-body aspect to aromatherapy. They speculate that the sweet lavender scent that reminds many humans of springtime or of grandmother's house doesn't offer the same connections for dogs.

When using aromatherapy for your dog, do not project human reactions onto canines. A scent that appeals to you may leave your dog flat. On the other hand, a scent that turns you off could delight an ailing dog. Valerian, for instance, which has an almost fecal smell to humans, may be used successfully to help dogs relax.

Holistic veterinarians don't use aromatherapy as a primary treatment modality, but as an adjunct. Many veterinarians use aromatherapy in conjunction with herbal and nutritional therapy. (For more information on aromatherapy for dogs, visit www.cybercanine.com)

PET TELEPATHY

Animal communicators believe that in the beginning, animals and plants communicated with one another through an energy accorded to all living creatures. Early humans were able to communicate with plants and animals via this same energy. Later, humans generally lost the conscious ability to communicate in this manner—although all humans can communicate this way if they recognize their abilities and reach an appropriate state of consciousness. Those who are conscious of the ability to interact with other creatures in this way are called animal communicators.

Animal communication can be used to heal the relationships between dogs and the people who interact with them—animal communicators never call these people "owners." What do animals have to tell us? A dog may wish to express an opinion about a new significant other in its caretaker's life, or a lost pet may call out to its owner via this energy. A dog may let its caretaker know that he'd like her to stay home more in the evenings or that he really prefers one kind of food to another.

At the heart of pet telepathy, or animal communication, is a belief that animals are spiritual beings, just as humans are. The word psychic, which is also used to describe communicators, comes from the Greek word *psyche*, meaning soul, or spirit. Professional animal communicators help people solve behavior problems involving their animals. They can help find lost dogs and help people with very sick dogs make medical decisions. They can ease the decision to stop treatment by receiving messages from a dear pet that its time has come to pass into spirit. They can also help people get through the period of mourning after a beloved dog's death.

Communication can take place either face to face or telepathically. Physical distance between communicator, dog, and human caretaker is irrelevant as communicators explain that the energy moving among them is not confined to a physical space. All animals have something to say and communicators only act as intermediaries. They do not interpret; they only translate.

You can learn to communicate with your dog yourself. The first step to telepathic contact is quieting your mind and becoming receptive to the emotional messages your dog is sending. Listening to your dog can be an enlightening experience. Your dog, after all, knows you very well. You may learn new things about yourself—through your dog's eyes.

A GUIDE TO AGE-RELATED
HEALTH PROBLEMS

Many factors influence the way your dog ages and the age-related diseases he's likely to contract. Genetic makeup, environmental conditions, quality of nutrition, lifestyle, and the level of preventive veterinary care your dog gets are among the most important factors.

Signs and Symptoms to Monitor as Your Dog Ages

- ❁ Decreased general health
- ❁ Increased thirst
- ❁ Loss of house-training
- ❁ Reduced activity
- ❁ Excessive panting
- ❁ Confusion and disorientation
- ❁ Less interaction

- ❁ Inability to recognize family
- ❁ Decreased hearing
- ❁ Sleeps more during the day
- ❁ Altered appetite
- ❁ Weight change
- ❁ Difficulty climbing stairs
- ❁ Increased stiffness

Your dog will (mercifully) never suffer from all the problems you'll read about in this section. In fact, many dogs reach a ripe old age without contracting any age-related disease. But, to be on the safe side, you must educate yourself about the problems older dogs frequently develop. In this section, you will find a guide to the most common age-related conditions and disorders.

Many factors influence the way your dog ages and the age-related diseases he's likely to contract. Genetic make-up, environmental conditions, quality of nutrition, lifestyle, and the level of preventive veterinary care your dog gets are among the most important factors. Dogs age a lot more quickly than humans, so it's a good idea to begin preventive care for age-related diseases when your dog is as young as five years old.

As your dog ages, you should schedule geriatric veterinary check-ups, annually or more often, depending on your dog's health. Most veterinarians recommend beginning geriatric checkups at age seven. The geriatric check-up should include blood and urine tests, chest x-rays, and an electro-cardiogram (EKG). Regular dental scaling at the vet's office and a good home maintenance program also become more important as the years advance. Veterinarians now know that good dental hygiene can significantly add to a dog's life expectancy by preventing the development of systemic infections, heart disease, and kidney disease.

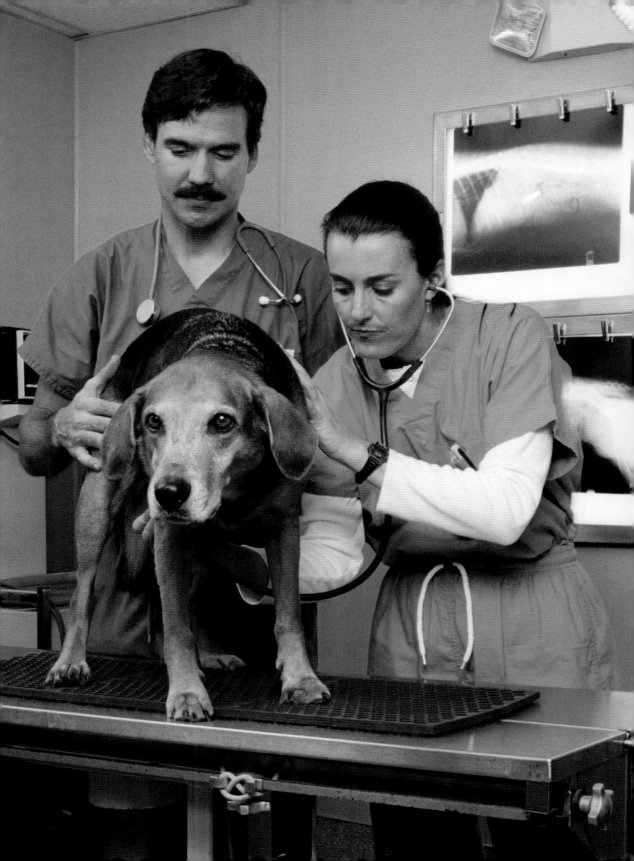

CHAPTER EIGHT

the most common age-related illnesses

To some extent, minor or major, your older dog will inevitably develop one of the following health problems. Fortunately, veterinary treatments for these diseases are helping older dogs cope much better than they did even a decade ago.

DIABETES

If your older dog has an insatiable thirst, and it seems she wants to go outside to urinate almost constantly, and she's having accidents in the house—especially at night—the most likely explanation is that she has developed diabetes mellitus, a pancreatic disorder that causes high blood sugar levels but, because of a lack of insulin, deprives the cells of the energy needed from sugar.

Diabetes mellitus, also called sugar diabetes, is by far the most common kind of diabetes that dogs develop. It's also a common problem for older humans. In healthy dogs (and humans), the pancreas produces insulin as part of the digestive process. Insulin aids in the digestion of sugars in food, helping the body store sugar as glycogen. Glycogen stores, in the liver and in the muscles, can be used as needed for energy. When insulin production drops, improperly digested sugar floods into the bloodstream and eventually shows up in the urine. This can cause dogs to spill urine in the house, especially at night.

The major signs of diabetes mellitus are:

- Increased urination
- Increased thirst
- Increased appetite
- Weight loss
- Muscle weakness
- Increased susceptibility to infections, especially urinary infections
- Poor healing

If the disease develops without treatment, these signs can develop:

- Diarrhea
- Vomiting
- Weakness
- Cataracts

Your veterinarian will diagnose diabetes based on a medical history, physical examination, and blood glucose tests done in the laboratory. Once it's established that your dog has diabetes, taking good care of her is the goal. There is no cure for diabetes mellitus, but dietary changes and insulin therapy can keep the situation under control in almost every case.

Managing diabetes means keeping your dog at a sensible weight and feeding her healthy food at regular intervals. It's important to feed your dog regularly so that the sugar in the food she eats can be digested and utilized without difficulty. Your veterinarian may recommend special kinds of foods that are suitable for diabetic dogs. Many dogs also need insulin injections, administered under the skin—usually twice a day—to keep blood glucose (sugar) levels regular.

Dogs with well-controlled diabetes can expect to live long and energetic lives. Taking good care of your dog is your responsibility. While dogs with controlled diabetes may eventually develop cataracts, they will not suffer the dangerous and life-threatening complications dogs with uncontrolled diabetes do.

OSTEOARTHRITIS

Osteoarthritis is a degenerative disease characterized by chronic pain, inflammation, and reduced mobility. It can affect dogs of all sizes, ages, and breeds, but it is more common in dogs seven years and older, and in larger breeds. Overweight dogs are at increased risk for osteoarthritis.

Stiff joints make it hard for dogs suffering from osteoarthritis to walk, run, and climb stairs. They are reluctant to jump and play. They may limp and yelp or

Symptoms of Osteoarthritis	
Mild	Slight stiffness and lameness when walking
	Mild pain if the affected joint is touched
	Licking of affected joint may occur
Moderate	Increased stiffness and lameness
	Shorter strides when walking
	Obvious pain if the affected joint is touched
	Occasional whining and/or whimpering
	Sitting preferred over standing
	Reluctance to climb steps or jump up
	Slow to rise from a resting position
Severe	Reluctance to rise or walk more than a few steps
	Dog will not allow affected joint to be touched
	Frequent whining and/or whimpering
	Frequent licking of affected joint
	Noticeable behavioral changes
	Increased difficulty in rising from a resting position

whimper when touched. Other symptoms include difficulty rising from a resting position and acting aggressive or withdrawn—which appears to be a personality change but is actually the result of chronic pain.

Osteoarthritis may be treated with traditional non-steroidal anti-inflammatory drugs (NSAIDs). Hydrotherapy can also help, and some veterinarians now prescribe nutritional supplements such as glucosamine sulphate or chondroitin sulphate, which are also used to treat osteoarthritis in humans.

KIDNEY DISEASE

Acute-onset kidney disease can afflict dogs at any point in their lives. In fact, the primary cause of acute renal failure in dogs is drinking antifreeze, stagnant water, or ingesting other harmful substances such as insecticides and some drugs. To prevent these potentially fatal accidents from happening, be sure to keep all dangerous household products safely out of your dog's reach.

Chronic renal failure is more likely to afflict older dogs, since it is the result of years of wear and tear on the kidneys. It is one of the most common medical problems of elderly dogs and a leading cause of death. Unfortunately, once kidney damage has occurred, it cannot be reversed. There are ways, however, to treat symptoms, to extend the dog's life and to make him more comfortable.

HOW KIDNEY DISEASE DEVELOPS

Your dog's kidneys, like your own, are filters that remove waste materials from the bloodstream. The kidneys also regulate the volume and the composition of your dog's body fluids. Signs of kidney problems are often not apparent until two thirds or more of the total kidney function has been lost.

The primary signs of chronic kidney disease are increased urination and increased thirst. As your dog ages and his kidneys become less efficient, his body compensates by increasing blood flow to the kidneys to try to improve the filtering process. As a side effect, however, your dog produces more urine. At the same time, he becomes dehydrated due to increased fluid loss in the urine. Thirsty, your dog begins to drink more and more water.

In cases of acute kidney disease, the symptoms can be markedly different. The dog produces little or no urine, doesn't want to drink any water, and becomes very lethargic. He may also vomit or develop diarrhea.

DIAGNOSIS AND TREATMENT

The signs of acute kidney failure are hard to miss. Once you've observed them, bring your dog to the veterinarian immediately. Chronic disease can be less obvious. As a result, some veterinarians include kidney function tests in annual examinations for older dogs.

Diagnosis involves blood and urine tests to determine how well the kidneys are filtering toxic substances from the blood. Once a dog is diagnosed with kidney disease, treatment begins. The goal of treatment is to get the kidneys functioning at their optimum potential and to maintain that functioning for as long as possible. The veterinarian may use intravenous fluids to flush out the system and to stimulate the kidneys to function better. A special diet—with reduced salt and protein—may also be recommended to take pressure off the kidneys. Your vet may also recommend potassium supplements and will

Signs of Urinary Tract Problems

The best thing you can do to help your dog in an emergency is to be prepared in advance. Here are some steps to take so you're always ready. Look out for the following. They may point to a urinary tract infection.

- ❧ Frequent urination
- ❧ Excessive thirst
- ❧ Unusual color or odor of urine
- ❧ Blood in the urine
- ❧ Straining and/or pain at urination
- ❧ Discharge from penis or vulva

urge you to keep fresh water available to your dog at all times.

URINARY TRACT PROBLEMS

Urinary tract troubles can develop at any age, but older dogs are much more prone to the bladder control problems that result in urinary incontinence. Drinking a lot of water and urinating a lot can be symptoms of a variety of diseases, diabetes and kidney problems among them. But age-related urinary incontinence may also be due to drops in hormone levels, particularly in female dogs. Your veterinarian can prescribe medication to strengthen your dog's sphincter muscles and bladder.

Older dogs can also suffer from urinary blockages. Most frequently, these blockages mean that stones have developed in the bladder or the urethra, making it painful for a dog to urinate. Stones are made up of minerals, such as salt or calcium, and they create tiny, pebble-like formations in the dog's bladder or urethra. Your veterinarian can treat the stones with a combination of drugs and surgery. Bladder stones may also be the culprit when dogs produce blood in their urine. Blood-tinged urine can also be a sign of a bladder infection, a kidney infection, or an injury to the urinary tract, so it's extremely important to see the veterinarian for diagnosis.

Female dogs are more prone to urinary tract infections than males are. In most cases, these are low-level bacterial infections that can be treated quickly and effectively with antibiotics. But urinary tract infections in males can be the sign of a more serious problem—prostatitis, an inflammation of the prostate gland. Left untreated, prostate gland infections can lead to sepsis (bloodstream poisoning). Symptoms of prostatitis include a stiff gait in the rear legs, fever, lethargy, and sometimes a urinary discharge. Dogs with prostate gland infection need to be taken to the veterinarian immediately. The veterinarian will diagnose the condition from physical examination, urinalysis, and a bacterial culture of the urine. Antibiotic treatment must be started right away to prevent sepsis.

CONSTIPATION

Although it's seldom a serious problem, constipation is a painful and irritating experience for many older dogs. The definition of constipation is infrequent or difficult passage of dry, hard stools. Dogs who are constipated strain and have difficulty passing feces. Constipation occurs when dogs don't drink enough water and when the diet has insufficient fiber. To be sure that what your dog is suffering is actually constipation, it's important to get a diagnosis from the veterinarian. A physical examination, including a digital rectal examination, is usually sufficient.

Once a diagnosis is made, and assuming that no blockage exists, the veterinarian will probably recommend an enema or a laxative to help empty the colon. In some cases, more than one enema will be necessary to soften the fecal mass and intravenous fluid therapy may be necessary for dogs who have become dehydrated as a result of constipation.

The best treatment for constipation, however, is preventive care. A diet rich in fiber is the most important way you can help prevent constipation. Non-digestible fiber increases water retention in the colon and this makes stools softer and easier to pass. The increased bulk of the fiber also improves muscle tone in the intestine, making it easier for the dog to move his bowels. Make sure your dog always has access to fresh, clean water. And include exercise in his daily routine. Regular exercise helps dogs digest and eliminate the food they eat.

EYE DISEASE

Your older dog depends on her eyes to keep her youthful and active. The eyes are sensitive organs, prone to a variety of diseases. A small amount of clear discharge from the eyes is normal, but if the discharge becomes profuse or takes on a strong coloration, see your veterinarian right away. Do not treat eye problems lightly. Damage can happen quickly if a problem goes untreated. Following are some of the more common eye problems your older dog may develop.

Conjunctivitis: An inflammation of the mucous membrane that lines the eye socket. The signs are red, puffy eyes and unusual discharge. Conjunctivitis can be caused by seasonal allergies or by tiny cuts or abrasions in the eye. This condition is easily cleared up with antibiotic eye drops or other medications.

Dry eye: This annoying problem can be a reaction to medication or simply a sign of aging. Older dogs may no longer have enough moisture in their eyes to tear up and keep the eyes clean and bright. Dry eye is often accompanied by a greenish-yellow discharge. Left untreated, it can lead to serious problems, including blindness. Talk to your veterinarian right away to find out what's causing the trouble. Ointments and eye drops to help stimulate the tear ducts are available.

Cataracts: Just like humans, dogs develop whitish discoloration of the lens of the eye that can block the passage of light through the lens. Dogs with cataracts look at the world through a fuzzy screen. The pupil, normally clear, develops a milky white appearance. Dogs with diabetes are more likely to develop cataracts than other dogs. Some breeds, including cocker spaniels, Bichons Frises, and poodles, are more susceptible than others. Treatment is surgical and dogs usually recover clear vision within a few weeks.

Glaucoma: Caused by excessive fluid pressure within the eye, glaucoma is a serious disease. Left untreated, it can lead to enlarged, protruding eyes and, eventually, to blindness. Symptoms include blue or gray discoloration of the eye, redness in the whites of the eye, vision loss, and pain. See your veterinarian right away if such symptoms develop. Caught in the early stages, glaucoma usually responds to medication, but surgery—and even removal of the eye—may be necessary as the disease progresses.

DENTAL PROBLEMS

As your dog gets older, his pearly whites start to yellow and his breath, never great to begin with, can make a good cuddle seem like a bad idea. In some cases, bad breath and discolored teeth can be signs of dental disease. Bacteria accumulate in unhealthy gums and can move from there into the bloodstream, contributing to the development of serious systemic diseases, including heart and kidney problems.

The best way to avoid dental problems is to keep your dog's mouth clean with regular brushing and periodic deep cleanings at the veterinarian's office. Brushing your dog's teeth doesn't have to be an ordeal. Make it part of playtime and your dog will enjoy the attention. Use a regular soft-bristled toothbrush or choose a "finger booty," a rubber thimble-like device, at a pet supply store. Your veterinarian can help you choose a toothpaste suitable for your pet. These special toothpastes have flavors that appeal to dogs and contain enzymes that break down dental plaque, and they can be swallowed—an important feature, since dogs can't spit. Don't use your minty-flavored toothpaste on your faithful companion: he won't like it and it won't do a proper job on his teeth. Begin with the large canine teeth and work toward the back of your dog's mouth. Focus on the outside surfaces of the teeth. Your dog's tongue keeps the inside surfaces of his teeth clean and free of plaque.

Inherited Illnesses and Conditions

Depending on what breed your dog is, he or she may be predisposed to certain health problems.

BREED	CONDITION
American Cocker Spaniel	Epilepsy
Bernese Mountain Dog	Shoulder lameness
Bichon Frise	Tartar formation and gum infection
Bull Terrier	Kidney failure
Cavalier King Charles Spaniel	Heart disease
Doberman	Heart disease
German Shepherd	Arthritis, eye disease, gastrointestinal disease
Golden Retriever	Eye problems, hip dysplasia
Great Dane	Hip and elbow problems, bone tumors
Labrador Retriever	Cataracts, arthritis
Mexican Hairless	Fragile skin susceptible to sunburn, cuts, and dryness
Papillon	Knee injuries
Shar Pei	Eye problems
West Highland White Terrier	Skin allergies
Wire Fox Terrier	Hearing problems
Yorkshire Terrier	Gum disease, respiratory problems

CHAPTER NINE

age-related diseases that are difficult to diagnose

Your veterinarian may need to be a detective to diagnose these elusive conditions. Knowing what the symptoms are, and what kinds of behavioral changes accompany these diseases, will help you bring your vet the necessary clues to solve the mystery. Your older dog can't tell you how he's feeling or where it hurts. It's your responsibility to pay attention to the signs and symptoms of illness. Whenever you are concerned about your dog's health, don't hesitate to make an appointment with your veterinarian. Only a trained veterinarian can diagnose and treat your dog's health problems.

CANCER

One in four dogs will develop cancer in its lifetime and almost half of all dogs over age ten eventually die from this disease. Age is the most important risk factor in the development of canine cancers and different breeds have a tendency to develop different kinds of cancer. Boxers and Scottish terriers, for instance, are prone to skin cancer. Very large dogs are at higher risk for bone cancer.

A tumor is any sort of lump, bump, growth, or swelling. Dogs can develop many kinds of tumors, some benign and some malignant, but the most likely places for cancer to develop include the skin and mammary glands, lymph nodes, mouth, and bones. Although more is being learned every day about what causes cancer and how it can be prevented and treated, the diagnosis remains a frightening one. Diagnosis can be difficult and the course of the disease is frequently unpredictable, involving a complex interplay between inherited traits and the environment. The earlier a cancer is caught, the better the prognosis will be.

When a veterinarian suspects that cancer is present, a biopsy, a microscopic examination of cells or tissues, is requested. A veterinary pathologist conducts the biopsy. When cancer is diagnosed, decisions must be made regarding treatment. Treatment options are much better than they were even ten years ago, but the decision-making process is still extremely difficult and cancer treatment can be quite expensive.

Surgery is often the first choice. It can be the quickest, least expensive, and most effective way to eradicate many types of cancer. Sometimes your regular veterinarian can do the surgery, but when surgery is difficult because a tumor is large or because there are many tumors, a specialist may be called in to perform the operation. There are risks associated with surgery and anesthesia, especially for older dogs. Faced with this kind of decision, you must weigh the pros and cons carefully with your veterinarian.

In some cases, radiation is the best choice, as an independent treatment or as an adjunct to surgery. Radiation helps prevent tumors from growing any larger or from spreading to other parts of the body and is particularly effective with certain kinds of tumors. The drawback is that radiation requires expensive equipment and must be done at a major medical center.

Warning Signs of Cancer

❧ Abnormal swellings that continue to grow, especially in the lymph nodes

❧ Sores that don't heal

❧ Bleeding or discharge from the mouth, nose, urinary tract, vagina, or rectum

❧ Offensive odor

❧ Difficulty eating and/or swallowing

❧ Difficulty breathing

❧ Difficulty urinating or defecating

❧ Hesitation to exercise, or loss of energy

❧ Loss of appetite, weight loss

❧ Persistent lameness or stiffness of movement

❧ Lumps in the breast area

❧ Abnormality or difference in size of testicles

Types of Heart Disease	
Valvular disease	Thickening of the heart valves causes them to leak blood as the heart pumps. Can lead to congestive heart failure. By far the most common form of heart disease in dogs.
Myocarditis	An inflammation of the heart muscle, often caused by a viral infection.
Pericarditis	An inflammation of the pericardial sack that surrounds the heart. Usually very dangerous.
Arrythmia	Irregular heart beats. These are caused by malfunctions in the heart's electrical system. Can usually be controlled with medication or with an artificial pacemaker.
Cardiomyopathy	An abnormality in the muscle walls of the heart.
Heart worms	These parasites, which can be up to a foot long, lodge in the right side of the heart causing numerous heart and circulatory problems.
Congenital heart disease	Some dogs are born with heart problems. Holes in the heart, deformed or missing valves, and abnormal vessels are some of the most common birth defects.

Chemotherapy is usually the treatment of choice only when the cancer is advanced and tumors have spread throughout the dog's body. The decision to use chemotherapy is not an easy one because the side effects of treatment are debilitating. Sometimes older dogs aren't hardy enough to undergo the regimen. Your veterinarian will help you make the best choice for you and your animal.

CUSHING'S DISEASE

Cushing's disease is a hormonal disorder. It develops when the adrenal gland produces too much cortisol and related hormones. A tumor in the adrenal gland or in the pituitary gland is usually what triggers this overproduction.

Middle-aged and elderly dogs are most likely to develop Cushing's disease, which can be very difficult to recognize in its early stages. The onset of Cushing's is very slow and many people mistake the symptoms for signs of normal aging. The signs are commonly: increased thirst and uri-

nation, increased appetite, tiredness due to muscle weakness, and a pendulous abdomen covered with hairless skin. This "pot belly" doesn't just mean that the dog is putting on weight; it's the result of an enlarged liver.

If you become concerned about a cluster of symptoms like these, talk to your veterinarian. There are specific tests to diagnose Cushing's disease. Hormone replacement therapy is usually the recommended treatment. When that doesn't work, veterinarians may try surgery to remove an adrenal tumor or radiation to shrink the size of the pituitary tumors. The good news is that when Cushing's disease is caught early enough, the prognosis for recovery is excellent.

CANINE COGNITIVE DYSFUNCTION

Dogs who develop canine cognitive dysfunction (CCD), similar to senile dementia in humans, suffer from behavioral changes that can easily be mistaken for ordinary aging. They are frequently tired and they show less

Does Your Dog Need Health Insurance?

Dog lovers spend billions each year on medical care for their beloved pets. Older dogs, like older humans, get sick more frequently and account for the bulk of these medical bills. More and more dog owners are signing up for pet health insurance. These policies can help you make difficult medical treatment choices without worrying about the expenses. Most pet insurers don't pick up the whole tab for your dog's medical expenses, but they typically take care of at least half the bill.

Pet insurance is just starting to catch on in the United States; as a result, there aren't many insurance companies out there yet. Among the best known are Pet Assure and Veterinary Pet Insurance (VPI). VPI has been in business the longest. Based in Anaheim, California, VPI offers major medical insurance to dog owners in most states and in the District of Columbia. The company offers five different plans, each covering the same ailments but varying in deductibles, payment limits, per incident limits, aggregate limits per year, and premium amounts. VPI and other insurers are also starting to offer well-care coverage, which includes annual physical examinations, vaccinations, teeth cleaning, and flea protection for an additional premium.

Pet Assure, basically an HMO for animals, started out in the New York City area and quickly expanded to the national level. Pet Assure's members pay an annual fee with discounts for multiple-pet households. In return, members receive discounts (usually 25 percent) on all services performed by participating veterinarians and animal hospitals. Discounts are also available for other services, such as grooming and training.

Pet Assure and VPI have begun marketing their services to employers to offer as part of group benefit packages. Pet insurance can be a lure for new hires who don't have children and don't expect to retire any time soon, but do want to offer the best possible care to their pets.

interest in food and exercise than they did before. They don't respond to commands as quickly as they once did. In fact, they seem to be going deaf or, at least, to be developing selective hearing. They seem confused and disoriented from time to time and they may feel strange in familiar surroundings.

As the condition progresses, dogs with CCD lose their ability to recognize familiar places and faces of family members. They may develop compulsive behaviors like pacing, circling, and floor licking; they may whine, whimper, and bark at nothing at all. Sleeping problems are common. Dogs with CCD may sleep all day and be up all night. Some dogs develop tremors. Many lose their housetraining. CCD can be a heartbreaking situation, and a difficult one for owners as well as their pets. Until recently, when CCD progressed into its later stages, euthanasia seemed to be the only course.

Today, however, many dogs respond well to several medications now available for the treatment of CCD. A veterinary check-up can rule out other causes for the puzzling and disturbing behaviors that characterize the disease. Once a diagnosis is made, the veterinarian will determine whether

the dog is a good candidate for pharmaceutical therapy. With the help of these new drugs, many dogs are back to normal within weeks.

HEART DISEASE

The American Veterinary Association estimates that one out of ten dogs suffers from some form of heart disease. The good news is that with better nutrition and medical care, dogs with heart disease are now living longer than ever before. With modern diagnostic techniques, heart disease has become a manageable problem in most cases.

Your dog's heart, just like your own, is a muscular pump. Its job is to circulate the blood through the lungs for re-oxygenation and then throughout the body to meet its metabolic needs. When the heart is not capable of performing this function efficiently, heart disease is suspected.

There are many different causes of heart disease. Defects in the heart valves and muscles, tumors, trauma, heart-worm infections, and deterioration of the blood vessels can all lead to heart failure. In dogs, left-side valvular disease is the most common. In many cases, leaky valves no longer shut properly and the heart's power to pump blood through the body is compromised. Smaller breeds of dogs are more vulnerable to this condition (called mitral valve prolapse in humans as well as dogs). Small dogs may have problems much earlier than larger dogs, but all varieties of dogs may develop mitral valve prolapse eventually.

By the time a dog reaches nine years old, she's more likely than not suffering from some kind of heart trouble. Stress, poor diet, obesity, and lack of exercise contribute to heart problems over a period of time so preventive care is important. And early detection can save your dog's life.

Here are the signs of heart disease you should be on the lookout for:

- Coughing. In one type of heart disease, fluid tends to collect in the lungs and this triggers a cough, especially during exertion.
- Shortness of breath.
- Rapid heart rate or very slow heart rate.
- Swelling of the abdomen or lower limbs.

At every check-up, your veterinarian listens to your dog's chest for heart murmurs (a sign of leaking valves), rate and rhythm abnormalities, and abnormal lung sounds. If something sounds suspicious, the veterinarian will order diagnostic tests that may include x-rays, ultrasound, blood and urine tests, and an electrocardiogram (EKG).

Most of the time, heart disease is treatable and manageable. Today's advanced veterinary care makes the prognosis good in most cases. With proper care the progression of the disease can be controlled or dramatically slowed. Treatment frequently involves a combination of dietary and drug therapy for the rest of the dog's life. Regular, moderate exercise is also very beneficial. Treated well, most dogs with heart disease go on to live long, active lives. The eventual cause of death is frequently something completely different from the heart disease that has been diagnosed and treated successfully.

DILATED CARDIOMYOPATHY

Certain large breeds—Doberman pinschers, boxers, Great Danes, and Irish wolfhounds, in particular—are susceptible to a kind of heart disease in which the heart muscle becomes weak and enlarged. To make matters worse, dilated cardiomyopathy has no special symptoms. It is frequently mistaken for a respiratory problem. So, if your large-breed dog continues to have breathing trouble

despite treatment for respiratory disease, ask your veterinarian to schedule an EKG. This is the only way to tell for sure if a dog is suffering from dilated cardiomyopathy.

CARDIAC ARRHYTHMIA

Is your dog offbeat? Many older dogs develop an irregular heartbeat that slows them down, tires them out quickly, and makes them more vulnerable to heart attack and heart failure. Fortunately, there are a variety of treatments to help these dogs get back in rhythm. The most common kinds of cardiac arrhythmia are tachycardia, a condition in which the heart beats too fast, and bradycardia, a condition in which the heart beats more slowly than it should. Normally, a dog's heart beats between sixty and eighty times per minute.

To diagnose a heart arrhythmia, some veterinarians use a Holter device, an instrument that measures the heartbeat for a period of twenty-four hours or longer. While testing is in progress, the dog wears a harness, which keeps the Holter device, a small machine resembling a tape recorder, in place. The veterinarian may also give the dog a dose of medication—a beta-blocker, calcium channel blocker, atropine, or digoxin—to help pinpoint the exact nature of the arrhythmia.

Sometimes an arrhythmia is caused by another medical problem. Fevers, chronic pain, lung disease, gastrointestinal disease, and electrolyte imbalances can each contribute to an arrhythmia. In these cases, treating the underlying problem should bring the heartbeat back to normal. When the arrhythmia is the underlying problem, veterinarians have an arsenal of medications from which to choose. When medications aren't effective, or when side effects make long-term use impractical, a pacemaker can help a dog's heart get back into rhythm. Pacemakers are expensive, costing $1,000 and up, but the results are often dramatic.

END STAGE ISSUES

Caring for an elderly dog teaches patience and compassion. The way your dog responds to your care teaches much about gentleness and trust.

CHAPTER TEN

coping with chronic disease

Your dog, who was once a stubborn, silly pup and then a bright, agile friend, has seen you through good times and bad. The relationship that began when you welcomed her into your home and set about training her to be part of your family has only grown stronger as the years have gone by. But when you make room in your heart for a dog, you do so with the knowledge that she will age more quickly than you will, and that you are likely to outlive her. You make a commitment to deal with the aging process and to see your pet through illnesses, acute and chronic. Paradoxically, the bond you share with your dog makes assuming this responsibility a challenge and a gift at the same time.

Caring for an elderly dog teaches patience and compassion. The way your dog responds to your care teaches much about gentleness and trust. Sometimes, the waning days of a dog's life can be time for making important decisions. In other cases, life makes all the decisions for you and all you can do is bear loving witness. Either way, you will grow as you guide your dog through the end stages.

Over the course of a lifetime, a dog has few illnesses for which hospitalization is necessary. Even after an acute episode or after surgery, your dog will recuperate at home. You may be intimidated at the idea of becoming your dog's nurse and providing home care night and day without any training, but the important thing to remember is that your veterinarian is always at the other end of the phone. And, although it can be hard work, caring for your ailing dog at home has its satisfactions. You may feel closer than you ever have before. Sick dogs usually get better faster when they are lovingly cared for in the comfort of their own homes. Here are some of the responsibilities you may expect to take on and guidelines for handling them comfortably.

SETTING UP THE SICK ROOM

Your convalescent dog needs a warm, comfortable bed, fresh water, nutritious food, and easy access to a toileting area. If your dog needs to be kept very quiet and still, you can set up a recovery pen. For a small dog, this can be as simple an arrangement as a large cardboard box, lined with clean, warm bedding. A child's playpen makes a perfect recovery room for a larger dog. Again, you'll want to line a sleeping area with warm blankets.

Body temperature can drop when a dog is ill and dogs with a fever can get the chills. Ask your veterinarian what kind of bedding to provide. A hot water bottle may also be soothing. Provide food and water bowls and newspapers in one corner of the recovery area in case of accidents. If you don't have a playpen, your dog's own crate makes a perfectly acceptable recovery space. The main thing is to keep the dog restricted. Dogs don't always know they're ailing and may be tempted to run around and overexert themselves.

MAKE SURE YOUR DOG'S NUTRITIONAL NEEDS ARE MET

Nursing a sick dog can be a challenge. Your dog won't understand why you need to poke and prod him as you administer treatments or take his temperature. Be sure to do everything as gently as you can, talking to your dog in a reassuring voice as you touch him. Some dogs lose their appetites when they don't feel well. Your veterinarian will ask you to be sure that your dog gets enough to drink to replace the fluids naturally lost each day. If your dog won't drink, you may need to try spooning water into the side of his mouth. A syringe or eyedropper can sometimes help an ailing dog drink more efficiently.

A dog who doesn't want to eat can often be tempted by food warmed to slightly above room temperature. Heating releases the scent of food and activates the dog's taste buds. Ask your veterinarian whether your dog should be on a special diet during the recuperative period. When there are no special dietary restrictions, try serving your dog's favorite foods to whet his appetite. Your vet may also recommend special nutritionally enhanced drinks for a dog that won't eat much.

KEEP RECORDS

Part of your job as home care nurse is to maintain a good record of your dog's recovery. You'll want to keep a record of how much your dog eats and drinks, the frequency of urination, and quality of bowel movements. Your veterinarian may ask you to take the dog's temperature each day. If so, you will want to record the daily thermometer reading. When your dog is taking medication—especially if there's more than one kind to administer—keeping a chart helps you be sure you're on schedule. You may also want to record any unusual occurrences such as vomiting or diarrhea. A well-kept medical record will help you and the veterinarian monitor your dog's progress.

You can photocopy the sample chart on the following pages or use it as a template to create one that better suits your particular needs.

TAKING YOUR DOG'S TEMPERATURE

Like the veterinarian, you will be using a rectal thermometer. It's much safer because your dog could bite an oral thermometer, releasing toxic mercury into his mouth at worst or at best destroying a digital thermometer. Prepare to take the temperature by shaking the thermometer so that the mercury column drops down below 99 degrees Fahrenheit (37.2 Celsius). If you're using a digital rectal thermometer, you're all set. Lubricate the tip of the thermometer with a petroleum jelly or another lubricant your vet recommends.

Hold the dog's tail up with one hand and insert the thermometer into the rectum with a firm, gentle push. With a small dog, you need only insert the thermometer about an inch to get an accurate reading. For a larger dog, you may need to insert the thermometer more deeply, about half of its length. (Ask your veterinarian to show you how.) The easiest way to take a dog's temperature is usually with the dog standing but it can also be done while the dog is sitting or lying down. To make the process simpler and to reassure your dog, it's nice to have another family member or a friend hold the dog gently and pet him while you're taking the temperature.

It should only take about a minute for the thermometer to register your dog's temperature. To read a mercury thermometer, roll it back and forth between your fingers until you can see the thin mercury column inside. The point where the column stops is the dog's temperature. Each large mark represents one degree, each small mark two tenths of one degree. The easier-to-use digital thermometer will give you a clear readout. Normal is usually

Medical Chart							
	DAY 1	DAY 2	DAY 3	DAY 4	DAY 5	DAY 6	DAY 7
Temperature							
Appetite							
Water intake							
Stool							
Urine							
Medications administered							
Miscellaneous							

Medical Chart							
	DAY 8	DAY 9	DAY 10	DAY 11	DAY 12	DAY 13	DAY 14
Temperature							
Appetite							
Water intake							
Stool							
Urine							
Medications administered							
Miscellaneous							

101 degrees Fahrenheit to 102.5 degrees Fahrenheit (38.3 to 39.2 Celsius).

GIVING YOUR DOG A PILL

If you've had your dog for many years, you have probably had to give him pills before. But to refresh your memory, the trick is to make sure he swallows them! Follow these steps for the best results:

1. Grasp your dog's muzzle with one hand and tilt his nose up to about a 45-degree angle.

2. Gently press inward on his upper lips. This should get him to open his mouth a bit.

3. Protect yourself by keeping the upper lips gently rolled between the dog's teeth and your fingers.

4. With your other hand, place the pill or pills on your dog's tongue, as far back as possible. (If your dog is so small that it's hard to get your fingers in his mouth, drop the pills over the back of the tongue, aiming as carefully as possible.)

5. Allow your dog to close his mouth while you keep his nose pointed upward for a moment. This seems to encourage swallowing.

6. Watch for your dog to lick his nose. That's a good sign that the pill has been swallowed.

Most dogs take pills pretty easily, but if your dog fights the pilling process, you can hide the pills in a bite of food, or crush the pill and mix it thoroughly into a small portion of food. Ask your veterinarian about this because the effects of some drugs change when they are mixed with foods and it's harder to tell whether the dog has taken all his medicine when it's consumed this way. If your dog has a prescription for a liquid medicine, administer it in the same way as you would a pill. Open his mouth, tip his muzzle upward, and, using a syringe or an eyedropper, squeeze the liquid into the dog's mouth. Aim for the area between the outside surfaces of the molar teeth and the inside surface of the cheek.

EARDROPS, EYEDROPS, AND EYE OINTMENTS

Dogs who are ailing frequently develop problems with their eyes or ears. You may be familiar with administering eardrops and eyedrops from earlier episodes of infection, but here is a refresher course in the process.

Eardrops: Hold your dog's head still, and, with the earflap laid back, insert the nozzle of the bottle in the ear in a forward direction toward the tip of the nose. Insert the appropriate number of drops into the ear. Now, without letting the dog shake his head, withdraw the bottle, drop the earflap back into position and, with the palm of your hand, gently but firmly massage the ear. This helps the medication lubricate the entire ear canal.

Eye drops: Gently restrain your dog and hold his eye open. Bringing your hand to the eye from above and behind so as not to frighten him, gently squeeze the proper number of eye drops into the eye. Allow the eye to bathe in the medication.

Eye ointment: Apply the ointment in a line along the inside of the lower eyelid. Do not let the applicator touch the dog's eye. Hold the dog's eye closed for a few seconds so that the ointment warms to the dog's body temperature and disperses over the eye. The eye will look greasy for a moment but should clear quickly.

TLC

The final ingredient, and sometimes the most important one, in any recuperative process—canine or human—is the tender loving care provided by caregivers. Spend time with your dog during his illness. Groom him carefully, pet him, and talk to him. Let him stay close to you while you read a book or watch television. You may want to let him sleep in your room at night. The love your dog feels from you will help him cope with his pain and discomfort.

CHAPTER ELEVEN

facing death

Your dog has been a loyal companion. She has a special place in your home and in your heart. When the time comes to say goodbye, there will be tears and sorrow. Many dogs die peacefully in their sleep without any suffering at all. But that isn't always the case. Sometimes you must decide whether to end your dog's life or allow a progressive disease to continue. This is never an easy decision. Veterinary advances today have resulted in effective new treatments for canine geriatric diseases. This progress is wonderful, but there are times when it can make the decision to let a dog go even harder than it used to be. Survival may be a possibility for a dog using new medical procedures and treatments, but an owner may be unable to afford the considerable expense involved. There are home care considerations, too. A dog who spends his last weeks and months in a deteriorated condition may need round-the-clock nursing care at home. If everyone works outside the home, this may put an untenable burden on the family. And finally, there are quality-of-life issues to consider. Helping your dog achieve a peaceful and dignified death is in many cases the most humane way to deal with a painful and debilitating illness.

One of the best things you can do is bring a trusted veterinarian into the decision-making process with you. Your veterinarian has vast experience with which to help you weigh the choices. The veterinarian will be able to help you understand your dog's level of suffering, which is the most important factor in any decision to euthanize. Some people keep their dogs alive longer than they should because they can't bear to say goodbye. But if a dog's suffering is intense, think about his pain before your own reluctance to let go.

You can get a good sense of how your dog is feeling and what her quality of life is like by making a list of the activities she has always enjoyed. Then, go down the list and consider how much or how little your dog is still getting pleasure out of life. Does she still enjoy her meals? Does she like to go for walks and play? Is she ever frisky anymore or does she spend most of her time lounging on the couch? Does she have trouble sleeping at night? Does she whine or moan in pain? Your dog may try her best to hide her pain from you, so it's important that you watch closely for signs that she is suffering.

The veterinarian can help you consider the options, but he or she can not make the decision to put your pet to sleep. That rests on your shoulders. Rest assured, you need not worry about your dog suffering any pain during euthanasia. It is a completely painless process. You are able to stay with your dog and hold her in your arms, if you wish. The veterinarian administers a lethal injection of an anaesthetic drug. Your dog will simply seem to go to sleep. Your veterinarian will discuss disposal of the remains with you before the euthanasia appointment. Local laws dictate whether and where dead pets can be buried. Veterinary hospitals often offer cremation services with or without return of the dog's ashes.

THE GRIEVING PROCESS

Losing someone or something you care about is painful. Grief is a normal process, with both physical and emotional signs. Like any other loss, the death of a beloved pet leaves a real hole in your life. Your grief can take many forms, including:

- Sadness and tears
- Not wanting to believe the loss is real (You may find yourself looking around for your dear pet, forgetting for a moment that she's gone.)
- Feeling angry
- Feeling that no one understands your grief
- Thinking you could have done something to save your dog
- Feeling guilty for being relieved that the suffering is over
- And finally, accepting that the loss is real and that you can cope with it

Losing a pet often triggers unresolved feelings about other losses, such as the deaths of family members or friends, a divorce, or the death of another pet. The feelings can be overwhelming. It's important to give yourself a break. Don't expect to accomplish too much in the first days and weeks after your dog's death. It may be hard to work, to

focus on your family, or to get involved in your usual activities for a while. Allow time for healing. Do some things that you enjoy. Go for a ride in the country. Read a good book. Go to see a happy movie.

You may have feelings of guilt if you have made a decision to have your dog euthanized. Veterinarians say that this is normal and that is the most loyal, loving dog owners, in fact, who feel the most guilty about this difficult decision. Take comfort in the knowledge that you made a good choice for your friend, a choice that spared her from unnecessary suffering.

People who are grieving the death of an animal have an extra burden to bear. Everyone understands grief when it involves losing a human, but there is often less compassion when it is an animal companion that is gone. The bereaved feels misunderstood and can be deeply hurt by casual comments such as, "Get over it. It was only a dog." In an effort not to seem too attached to a "mere" animal, some people try to minimize the loss even to themselves. Don't deny your legitimate feelings of loss. Allow yourself to experience the sorrow in your own way.

TALKING TO CHILDREN ABOUT A PET'S DEATH

For many children, the death of a beloved dog may be the first experience they have with death. In many cases, the child has lived with this pet all his life and has become closely attached to him. Most children see the family pet as "my" dog and the relationship can be almost like a sibling relationship, especially for an only child. It's very important, therefore, to keep your child involved in the process of bereavement.

Be honest with your child about an older dog's illness. Encourage your child to be part of the home care team in an age-appropriate way. Your child can help feed an ailing

dog and spend time comforting a dog who isn't feeling well. This participation in care will help the child deal with grief after the dog dies. The child can feel that he's done his part to help ease his friend's last days and hours.

If a decision is made to euthanize the dog, make sure that the child knows what's going on. Many veterinarians welcome children into their offices for the euthanasia and encourage them to be with their pets as they die. This can be a very touching experience. Often everyone, children and adults including the veterinarian—go through the process in tears. Your child can develop a reservoir of compassion from being a witness to this gentle death.

However, you may want to check with a child psychologist or social worker, depending on the age of your child, about whether or not the child should be present at the euthanasia. Some children are old enough at six or seven; others are too vulnerable at ten or twelve. You don't want to push your child into an experience he isn't ready for yet. A child who is too young to be present at euthanasia can say goodbye to the dog at home. There are some very good picture books available for young children who have lost pets. Ask your veterinarian to recommend one. Reading one of these books together can be comforting.

WHERE TO FIND SUPPORT

When the loss of your faithful companion is too much to bear, you can find help and understanding through one of the pet loss support hotlines that have been set up by veterinary schools and veterinary associations across the country. These hotlines are open to all pet owners and not just to veterinary hospital clients. You will find someone to talk to, usually a trained grief counselor, who can help you deal with your loss. The loss of a pet can be magnified, counselors say, when the grieving person lives alone. There are also times when no one in the family, not even a spouse, can understand what you're going through. At other times, the loss is compounded by another loss. Grief counselors say they get calls from dog owners who have lost a human loved one and a canine companion in a short time period. The combination can be overwhelming.

Pet Loss Hot Lines

The following is a list of some of the larger pet loss hotlines operated by veterinary schools with their hours of operation:

❖ **Chicago Veterinary Medicine Association**
Lines are open from 7 pm to 9 pm, central time, Monday through Friday.
630-603-3994

❖ **Colorado State University Veterinary Teaching Hospital**
Lines are open from 9 am to 5 pm, mountain time, Monday, Tuesday, Thursday, Friday.
970-491-1242

❖ **Cornell University Pet Loss Support Hotline**
Lines are open from 6 pm to 9 pm, eastern time, Tuesday, Wednesday, Thursday.
607-253-3932

❖ **University of Florida, School of Veterinary Medicine**
Lines are open from 7 pm to 9 pm, eastern time, Monday through Friday.
352-392-4700. At prompt, dial 1, then 4080.

❖ **Michigan State University School of Veterinary Medicine**
Lines are open from 6:30 pm to 9:30 pm, eastern time, Tuesday, Wednesday, Thursday.
517-432-2696

❖ **Ohio State University School of Veterinary Medicine**
Line are open from 6:30 pm to 9:30 pm, eastern time, Monday, Wednesday, Friday.
614-292-1823

❖ **Tufts University School of Veterinary Medicne**
Line are open from 6 pm to 9 pm, eastern time, Monday through Friday.
508-839-7966

❖ **University of California School of Veterinary Medicine**
Lines are open from 6:30 pm to 9:30 pm Pacific time, Monday through Friday.
916-752-4200

CHAPTER TWELVE

the future

After the loss of your beloved pet, your life may feel different in major ways. Loss brings with it a time for grief. With acceptance, the support of a few good listeners, and the passage of time, healing will gradually take place. In the meantime, you may be hurt and offended when people urge you to run right out and get a new dog as if simply replacing the dog you've lost would be the end of your grieving. Some dog owners themselves believe that the solution is to replace the dog they've lost immediately. They show up, still in tears, at the animal shelter or at a breeder's kennels. They want a dog just like the dog they lost. What they may really want is their old dog back, something they unfortunately can't have. Other bereaved dog lovers swear they will never let another animal into their heart because the loss has hurt them so much. For most people, the best approach lies somewhere in the middle. It just makes sense to wait a little while before you think about getting a new pet. Those who replace a beloved dog immediately will probably look for his traits and habits to show up in the new dog, but this will not happen because every dog is an individual. You don't want to be disappointed—nor do you want to see ordinary differences between one dog and another as behavioral problems. A little distance will help you start over again.

After a month or so, most people are ready to begin looking for a new pet with open hearts and reasonable expectations. But there are some people who will take much longer before sharing their homes with a new dog. This is fine and normal, too. You are the only who knows when the time is right. Your relationship with the dog you've lost may have been so close that you will not want to own another dog again. You may want to think about a cat as a pet or you may want to take time out from having pets in your life. If you have children, you will, however, be badgered into getting a new dog almost immediately and pretty much constantly. Children are not renowned for their ability to be patient so you may need to be firm with them. Never bring any pet into your home simply because your child has been pleading for one. That's a recipe for disaster. Soon, your child's enthusiasm will wane and you will be doing all the care taking, which may make you feel resentful. A dog needs lots of care and love and will quickly pick up your ambivalence and resentment.

Wait until you're ready before you even begin looking for a new dog. As you give yourself time to heal, you will also allow the scent of your old pet to fade from your house. This will make life easier for your new dog, who will not be puzzled by the scent-presence of an invisible dog. Let time heal and give your new dog the chance to show you his own special qualities.

WHAT TO DO WHEN YOU'RE READY

Most people who have enjoyed a long, loving relationship with a dog who has passed away will eventually want to share their home again. As you begin to look for a new canine companion, be ready to do a little research. Your search for a new pet may take you to animal shelters, to kennel clubs, to responsible breeders, and breed rescue clubs. Stay away from pet shops, however. That doggie in the window may look appealing, but he was probably bred in a puppy mill with little or no consideration for breeding characteristics, health care, or opportunities for proper socialization. Not only does this mean that the puppy may grow into a difficult dog, but, by buying a dog from a pet shop, you inadvertently support these unscrupulous puppy mill operators. Boycott them!

Your first decision is what kind of a dog to choose. Are you looking for the same breed or a similar mix? Or does the idea of a totally different kind of dog appeal to you? Breeders say that the most important element in establishing a long, loving relationship between dogs and humans is making the right match up front. Think carefully about what you want from your new dog.

- How will this dog fit into your life?
- What role will she play in your family?
- Has your lifestyle changed significantly since you brought your last dog home?
- Are you living in a different kind of housing?
- Have you moved from an urban to a rural area, or vice versa?
- Are you around the house more? Less?
- Are there more or fewer people in your family now?
- Do you know how much exercise and running outside you will be able to offer the new dog?
- Do you travel more or less than you did before?

The way you answer each of these questions will have an important impact on your search process. The last thing you want to do is buy or adopt a new dog on a whim. Too many people do this, especially when they are grieving and vulnerable to the charms of a sweet puppy or an abandoned dog at the local shelter. Think twice. You are a dog lover—that's established. But remember that you'll be starting over with all the responsibilities as well as the pleasures: the training process, the daily and weekly grooming sessions, and all the other commitments you will be taking on again.

Before you settle on a breed or a particular dog, do some background checking. Read books and magazines about the breeds that interest you. Ask your veterinarian for his or her opinion about what kind of dog would best suit you. Talk to people at kennel clubs, and to trainers, groomers, and breeders. If you know someone who has the kind of dog you're interested in, spend some time with that dog and get to know its characteristics. Ask questions. Is the breed considered easy to train? Does it require extensive grooming or does its high energy level require active outdoor exercise? Don't let anyone—including family members—pressure you into making a decision before you're ready. The reason most dogs wind up in shelters is because their owners acted impulsively and didn't consider the implications of owning a dog before they brought one home.

DO YOU WANT A PUPPY?

There are few things on earth more adorable than the antics of puppies. Puppies are also too young to have developed bad habits. You will be the first and only trainer. Yes, you'll have to housebreak the pup and teach him the obedience basics, but you will be able to train him to do things just as you want. You won't be working with behaviors and habits left over from someone else's efforts.

Once you've decided that a puppy's the dog for you, how do you go about choosing the right one? Breeders recommend considering the following:

Does the puppy come when called? Set him down, step back, and call while clapping softly, hands at puppy level. A pup who comes at once will be people-oriented and should be easy to train. One who wanders off will be independent. A pup who runs away from you will probably always be fearful.

OBEDIENCE

Gently roll the pup on his back and hold him there for thirty seconds. Have someone time you or silently count to yourself. Use both hands, wear a neutral expression, keep your head above the pup, don't speak and don't allow him to brace his feet against you. A docile pup will relax and lie still. A fearful pup will lie still without relaxing. An easy-to-train pup will struggle briefly, then lie still. A willful pup will struggle for the full thirty seconds. A domineering pup will scratch and nip at you.

TEMPERAMENT

Once the thirty seconds are over, continue to crouch beside the puppy, let him roll over and stand or sit in front of you. Gently place one hand on his chest and lightly stroke him from head to tail with the other. If the pup is calm and relaxed, bend your face close to him. A well-adjusted pup will recover quickly from being rolled over and may wag his tail, kiss your face, or try to climb into your lap. A frightened pup will take several minutes to recover and may be hesitant, and with ears and tail down, freeze in place or avoid you. Watch out for a pup who tries to jump at your face, who growls and tries to bite.

Important Questions to Ask Breeders, Rescuers, and Shelter Staff

❧ How big will he grow? (If you are considering a puppy)

❧ How much does she eat?

❧ How much exercise does he need?

❧ How often does she need to be groomed?

❧ What is the breed's traditional function? If the dog is a mixed breed, what's in the mix?

❧ Does he get along well with children?

❧ Is she playful?

❧ How much room does she need? Can she manage in an apartment, or does she need a big backyard?

❧ Does he shed? How much?

❧ What health problems are common to this kind of dog?

❧ Does she get along with other dogs? With cats?

❧ Is he/she neutered or spayed?

❧ How has the puppy or dog been socialized?

CHOOSING AN EXPERIENCED DOG

If your house is empty much of the day or you no longer have the patience and energy to go through the training process with a puppy, a young adult dog may be the perfect choice for you. With this choice, you will have the satisfaction of knowing that you are offering a loving home to a dog who has been abandoned by previous owners. Ask your veterinarian, local trainers, and groomers where they recommend looking for older dogs.

Many breeds have rescue organizations working toward the placement of abandoned and neglected dogs. The American Kennel Club keeps a list of U.S. rescue organizations. You can also find them on the World Wide Web. Most have local and regional chapters.

The other obvious choice for finding an adult dog is your local shelter. Some of the sweetest, most beautiful dogs in the world come from shelters. Keep your heart off your sleeve when you visit, however. It's a good idea to keep going back to a shelter repeatedly before deciding on a dog to adopt. Remember, you are making a serious, long-term decision. Don't get caught up in emotion when you see dogs in cages, whining and crying and looking pitiful. Taking your time to be sure that the match is a good one is the kindest and most helpful thing you can do for the dog as well as for you.

The advantage of choosing an older dog is that she will probably be trained and housebroken. However, she may also have developed a bad habit or two over the years. The good news is that most trainers say you can teach an old dog new tricks—as long as you're patient and willing to put in the time. Just beware the dog who has been placed in the shelter because he is mean, dominating, or excessively fearful. Unfortunately, shelter operators don't always know everything about their charges' backgrounds.

You will need to fall back on your instincts, and whatever advice you can get from your veterinarian, to gauge the shelter dog's temperament.

CHECKING YOUR NEW DOG'S HEALTH STATUS

When you buy a puppy from a breeder, you will be given records and other documents attesting to the dog's good health. An adult dog adopted from a rescue club should also come with papers, and may have spent time in a foster home being monitored for health problems as well as behavioral traits. The dog who comes from a shelter does not have these advantages. But whether your dog comes with a pedigree, a health history, or nothing at all, you must make an appointment to take him for a veterinary check-up as soon as possible. Only after your veterinarian has given your new dog a clean bill of health can you be sure that everything's okay. Here are some of the signs your veterinarian will be looking for when she examines your new canine companion:

- Bright, shiny eyes with little or no discharge or watering. Whites of the eyes white, not red.
- A cool, moist nose that isn't running
- Firm gums and clean-smelling breath
- Ears free of wax or odor
- A good gait that doesn't favor any paw or leg
- Clean and glossy coat
- Smooth skin, free of parasites

BRINGING YOUR NEW DOG HOME

Introducing your dog to his new home is a joyful experience. You'll have fun watching him sniff around and explore his surroundings. You may want to make special provisions for the first night in the house, however. Let your new dog bring a memento from his old home, even if it's just a piece of toweling from the shelter, so he'll have something familiar to smell when he goes to sleep at

night. If you don't have a crate already, you may want to invest in one, especially if you are starting over with a puppy. The dog will actually feel safer and more comfortable sleeping in a crate in strange surroundings. He may also want to sleep close to you. That's your decision. Let the dog sleep in your bedroom if you're comfortable with that. Don't do it if you have allergies or trouble sleeping. Whatever you do from the beginning will be starting a pattern and forming a habit.

If your old dog was quiet and slept a lot, you may be surprised at how curious and energetic your new dog is. So,

dog-proof your home in anticipation. Take a good look around and see whether your home is safe for your new dog and whether all the things you treasure are safe from the new dog. Keep all toxic cleaning materials stored away with childproof locks on the cabinet doors. Make sure your trash cans have tight-fitting lids and empty them frequently, unless you want the dog to empty them for you. Survey your rooms for knickknacks, fragile lamps, and other breakables. Put them away for the time being or move them up to higher ground where your dog won't be able to get at them. Don't leave jewelry, art supplies, puzzle pieces, or knitting, sewing, or any other hobby materials lying around to tempt the new dog. Find a place for everything and put it all away. Tuck electrical cords out of sight, especially if you're bringing a puppy home— and don't leave your slippers on the floor in front of your favorite chair. Put them away until your new pup has passed through the stage when he wants to chew everything in sight.

Today is the beginning of your lives together. Gather all the family members for a quiet celebration of the newest member. Make your new dog feel at home. Of course, you will always remember your older dog and any other pets who've shared your home. You'll probably keep at least one photograph prominently displayed even as you're starting over with a new dog. You will always cherish the love and friendship you enjoyed. But now it's time to invest that kind of energy in your new friend. As you get to know each other, and learn to understand and love each other, you will discover how lucky you are to have another best friend.

RESOURCES

ASSOCIATIONS

Academy for Veterinary Homeopathy
1283 Lincoln Street
Eugene, OR 97401
541-342-7665

American Animal Hospital Association
P.O. Box 150899
Denver, CO 80215-0899
303-986-2800

American Dog Owners Association
1654 Columbia Turnpike
Castleton, NY 12033

American Holistic Veterinary Medical
 Association
 2214 Old Emmorton Road
Bel Air, MD 21015
410-569-0795

Animal Behavior Society
Dept. of Physiology
Campus P.O. Box 173364
Denver, CO 80217-3364

Baker Institute for Animal Health
 College of Veterinary Medicine
Cornell University
Ithaca, NY 14853

Center for Veterinary Acupuncture
1405 West Silver Spring Drive
Glendale, WI 53209
414-352-0201

Endangered Dogs Association
P.O. Box 1544
London W7 2ZB
England
0181-843-9751

International Association for Veterinary
 Homeopathy
334 Knollwood Lanne
Woodstock, GA 30188
404-516-5954

International Veterinary
 Acupuncture Society
P.O. Box 66579
Nedeerland, OR 80466
303-258-3767

Veterinary Institute for
 Therapeutic Alternatives
15 Sunset Terrace
Sherman, CT 06784
860-354-2287

GENERAL DOG CATALOGS

Bach Flower Remedies
644 Merrick Road
Lynbrook, NY 115563
516-593-2206

Dogwise
Direct Book Service
P.O. Box 15357
Seattle, WA 98115
800-776-2665

Doggone Good!
Innovative Products
8006602665

Dog Lovers Bookshop
9 West 31ST Street, 2ND Floor
New York, NY 10001
212-594-3601 phone
212-5764-343 fax

RESOURCES

The Dog's Outfitter
Home Pet Shop
Humboldt Industrial Park
1 Maplewood Drive
Hazelton, PA 18201-9798
800-FOR-DOGS

J & J Dog Supplies
P.O. Box 1517
Galesburg, IL 61402
800-642-2050

Premier Pet Products
2406 Krossridge Road
Richmond, VA 23236
800-933-5595

Whiskers Holistic Products for Pets
235 East 9th Street
New York, NY 10003
800-WHISKERS

MAGAZINES AND NEWSLETTERS

American Journal of Veterinary Research
Journal of the American Veterinary
  Association
American Veterinary Medical Association
930 N. Meacham Rd.
Schaumburg, IL 60196

Canine Chronicle
4422 Orange Grove Drive
Houston, TX 77039

Dogs, Dogs, Dogs!
2424 Danforth Avenue, Box 10 1
Toronto, Ontario M4C IK9
Canada
416-465-4406 phone
416-465-1513 fax

Dog Fancy
P.O. Box 53254
Boulder, CO 80322-3264

Dog News
Harris Publications
1115 Broadway
New York, NY 100 10

Dog World (USA)
29 North Wacker Dr.
Chicago, IL 60606

Dog World (Britain)
9 Tufton Street
Ashford, Kent TN23 IQN
England

Fetch the Paper
Pawprince Press
815 Clark Road
Mablemount, WA 98267
360-873-4333

Good Dog! Magazine
P.O. Box 10069
Austin, TX 78766
800-968-1738

North American Dog
Dogs International
P.O. Box 2270
Alpine, CA 919032270
800-364-3283

Pet Life
1227 West Magnolia Ave.
Forth Worth, TX 76104
800-767-9377

RESOURCES

GRIEF COUNSELORS

Charlene Dougloas, MS, Ph.D.
The Rainbow Passage
Pet Loss Support and Bereavement Center
1528 E. River Road
Grafton, WI 53024
414-376-0340

Barbara Myers
Holistic Animal Counseling Centre
718-720-5548

PetFriends
800-404-PETS

Pet Loss Foundation
Suite A23
1312 French Rd.
Depew, NY 14043
513-932-2270

Martha M. Tousley, R.N., M.S.
Bereavement Counselor
9818 East Ironwood Drive
Scottsdale, AZ 85258

SUGGESTED READING

GENERAL CARE

Bordwell, Sally. *The American Animal Hospital Association Encyclopedia of Dog Health and Care.* Quill, 1996.

Bower, John and Caroline Bower. *The Dog Owner's Problem Solver.* Reader's Digest, 1998.

Bown, Deni. *101 Essential Tips: Dog Care.* DK Publishing, 1995.

Copeland, Sue and John Hamil. *Hands-on Dog Care.* Doral Publishing, 2000.

Dennis, Helen. *101 Questions Your Dog Would Ask: What's Bothering Your Dog and How to Solve Its Problems.* Barrons Educational Series, 1999.

Fogle, DVM, Bruce. *The Complete Illustrated Guide to Dog Care.* Bay Press, 1994.

Klever, Ulrich. *The Complete Book of Dog Care: How to Raise a Happy and Healthy Dog.* Barrons Educational Series, 1989.

Lane, Marion S. *The Humane Society of the United States Complete Guide to Dog Care.* Little, Brown & Company, 1998.

Larkin, DVM, Peter. *Complete Guide to Dog Care (Practical Handbook Series).* Lorenz Books, 1998.

Woodhouse, Barbara. *Barbara Woodhouse on Keeping Your Dog Healthy.* Ringpress Books Ltd., 1994.

FIRST AID, MEDICAL, AND HEALING

Allport, Richard. *Heal Your Dog the Natural Way.* IDG Books Worldwide, 1997.

Bamberger, DVM, Michelle. *Help: The Quick Guide to First Aid for Your Dog.* IDG Books Worldwide, 1993.

Carlson, Delbert G. *Dog Owner's Home Veterinary Handbook.* IDG Books Worldwide, 1999.

Foster, Race. *Just What the Doctor Ordered: A Complete Guide to Drugs and Medications for Your Dog.* IDG Books Worldwide, 1996.

Hoffman, Matthew (editor). *Symptoms & Solutions: The Ultimate Home Health Guide— What to Watch For, What to Do (Dog Care Companions).* Rodale Press, 1999.

Lane, Dick. *A-Z of Dog Diseases & Health Problems: Signs, Diagnoses, Causes, Treatment.* IDG Books Worldwide, 1997.

SUGGESTED READING

Redding, Ph.D., Richard W. *The Dog's Drugstore: A Dog Owner's Guide to Nonprescription Drugs and Their Safe Use in Veterinary Home-Care.* St. Martin's Press, 2000.

Streitfredt, Uwe. *Healthy Dog, Happy Dog: A Complete Guide to Dog Diseases and Their Treatments.* Barrons Educational Series, 1994.

FEEDING
Anson, Suzan. *Bone Appetit: Gourmet Cooking for Your Dog.* New Chapter Press, 1989.

Bastedo, Alexandra and Jeannie Kemnitzer. *Canine Care & Cuisine: The Healthy Dog Book.* Robson Books Ltd., 1999.

Goss, Ellen. *The Best Fed Dog in America: Canine Cuisine, Dog Culture, Facts & Merriment.* Owl Bay Publishers, 1995.

Palika, Liz. *The Consumer's Guide to Dog Food: What's in Dog Food, Why It's There, and How to Chose the Best Food for Your Dog.* IDG Books Worldwide, 1995.

ALTERNATIVE METHODS
Buckloe, Jane. *How to Massage Your Dog.* Foster City, California: IDG Books Worldwide, 1995.

Hoffman, Matthew (editor). *Dogspeak: How to Understand Your Dog and Help Him Understand You (Dog Care Companions).* Rodale Press, 1999.

Levy, Juliette De Bairacli. *The Complete Herbal Handbook for Dog and Cat.* Faber & Faber, 1995.

Messonnier, Shawn. *The Allergy Solution for Dogs: Natural and Conventional Therapies to Ease Discomfort and Enhance Your Dog's Quality of Life.* Prima Publishing, 2000.

Messonnier, Shawn. *The Arthritis Solution for Dogs: Natural and Conventional Therapies to Ease Discomfort and Enhance Your Dog's Quality of Life.* Prima Publishing, 2000.

Volhard, Wendy and Kerry L. Brown. *The Holistic Guide for a Healthy Dog.* IDG Books Worldwide, 1995.

INDEX

A
Academy of Veterinary Homeopathy, 85
acupuncture, 69–70
additives, in food, 40
adoption, of new dog, 126–132
agility training, 52
aging
    illnesses related to, 21–22, 92–109
    onset of, 19, 90
    process of, 16–23
American Veterinary Chiropractic Association, 80
anemia, 28
anesthesia, weight and, 42
Animal Protection Institute, 39
antioxidants, 44
appetite loss, 29, 30, 114
aromatherapy, 85–86
arrhythmia, 109
arthritis, 29, 32, 42, 44
Association of American Feed Control Officials, 37–38
asthma, 27
Ayurveda, 70, 72–73

B
Bach, Dr. Edward, 73
Bach flower remedies, 73–74
balance, ears and, 27
behavior problems, 18, 29, 32
bites
    animal, 55–56
    insect, 60
    snake, 60
bleeding, 60

bones, of dog
    aging of, 32
    treating broken, 56
    see also chiropractic
bones, to chew, 45, 57
bowels, see constipation; diarrhea
bronchitis, 27
butylated hydroxyanisole (BHA), 40
butylated hydroxytoluene (BHT), 40

C
cancer, 101, 103
canine infectious tracheo-bronchitis, 27
cardiac arrhythmia, 109
cardiopulmonary resuscitation (CPR), 61–62, 64
cataracts, 18, 25, 98
chemotherapy treatment, 103
children, pet's death and, 122, 124, 127
Chinese medicine, 74, 76
chiropractic, 79–80
choking, 57, 60
cholesterol, 44
circulatory system, aging of, 28
Co-enzyme Q-10, 44
cognitive dysfunction disorder, 30, 32, 104, 106
communication, with dog, 85, 86
congestive heart failure, 28
conjunctivitis, 98
constipation, 42, 96
coughs, 27, 28
CPR, 61–62, 64
Cushing's disease, 103–104

cuts, treating, 55–56

D
death, of dog
    children and, 122, 124, 127
    decisions about, 86, 120–122
    grief about, 122, 124–125, 126
dental hygiene, see teeth
diabetes, 29, 42, 92–93
diarrhea, 29, 33, 40
diet, see food
digestive system, 30, 60
dilated cardiomyopathy, 109
dogs
    adopting new, 126–132
    benefits of owning, 12–13
    checklist for healthy, 23
doshas, 72, 73
dry eye, 98

E
ears
    aging of, 18, 25, 27, 29
    drops for, 118
    foreign objects in, 59
    mites in, 27
elimination, see constipation; diarrhea; urination
emphysema, 27
ethoxyquin, 40
euthanasia, 121–122, 124
exercise
    agility training and, 52
    basics of, 48, 50
    importance of, 46–48
    modifying, 29, 48
    parks for, 52

ABOUT THE AUTHOR

Dog lover, author, and freelance health writer Jean Callahan has contributed to five books and written articles for *Self, Glamour, Parenting,* and other national magazines. She has also written and produced many news letters on health and pets. She lives in Salem, Massachusetts.